OVERCOMING COMPULSIVE GAMBLING

A self-help guide using cognitive behavioral techniques

Alex Blaszczynski

Robinson
LONDON

Robinson Publishing Ltd
7 Kensington Church Court
London W8 4SP

First published by Robinson Publishing 1998

A copy of the British Library Cataloguing in Publication Data for
this title is available from the British Library.

ISBN 1-85487-484-5

Important Note
This book is not intended to be a substitute for medical advice or
treatment. Any person with a condition requiring medical
attention should consult a qualified medical practitioner or
suitable therapist.

Printed and bound in Great Britain by
Clays Ltd, St Ives plc

3 5 7 9 10 8 6 4 2

Contents

Contents

Acknowledgments

This self-help guide is based in large part on the theories of learning which form the foundation of cognitive and behavioral clinical psychology. The approach to managing problem gambling around which this guide to recovery is written is derived from many years of researching a broad range of impulse control disorders and in particular working with clients who suffer severe gambling problems. The essential core of our treatment guide is a relaxation technique called 'imaginal desensitization'. This technique has been successfully modified and applied to what we call impulse-driven behaviors by the eminent Australian psychiatrist Professor Nathaniel McConaghy MD, DSc. ('Impulse-driven' is a term used to refer to repetitive behaviors which are in some respects pleasurable but result in harm, whether to the person performing them, to his or her close associates and family members, or to others.) This work was carried out in Sydney, Australia, at the Prince of Wales Hospital Psychiatric Unit, which is part of the University of New South Wales teaching hospitals complex.

I am enormously indebted to Professor McConaghy for his guidance and support throughout the years of our association. I have learned much from this scholar, gaining an immeasurable respect for his intellectual rigor and the methodological precision which he applied to his research work, and the clinical acumen and genuine care displayed in the management of his patients. From the beginning of my career to the present day, he has been my mentor and source of inspiration.

This book has been beaten and moulded into its final form

through the contributions of many people: academics, friends and laymen. I am especially thankful to all the gamblers who have, through their suffering, given me a greater understanding of the complexities underlying the mechanism of self-control.

A number of valued colleagues and friends, notably Derrick Silove, Vijaya Manicavasagar and Sue Cremer, have provided constructive criticism and astute advice and have devoted time and energy to reading and editing the manuscript. In particular, I would like to thank Jackie Curtis for providing insightful comments and suggestions on improving the quality of the self-help guide in Part Two.

I must thank Peter Cooper for his recognition of the need for a self-help book on problem gambling and for his endeavours on my behalf to convince the editors of the value of this book.

In all, I thank my wife Pamela and sons Kristian and Stefan for their generous support and love; and my parents, brother and grandmother for their direction and encouragement in life.

Preface

We know that, for many adults, gambling is a form of entertainment in which they play hoping to win but, in reality, expecting to lose. We are not concerned with these people. This book is intended to help all those who have lost control over their gambling to such an extent that it has caused major problems in their life. Such problems may affect their own psychological well-being, causing depression, anxiety and drug and alcohol abuse; interfere with their ability to work productively or hold down a job; lead to marital friction; or impel the gambler to carry out crimes in support of the habit. For such people, the urge to gamble is often so great that the gambler becomes almost totally obsessed with thoughts of the next bet and where to find the money to stake. The dream of untold wealth and the need to win to pay off debts add fuel to the fire. So strong is this desire that all else pales into insignificance.

The guide to recovery in Part Two of this book offers gamblers step-by-step instruction in how to regain control over their behavior and beat the gambling bug. We know the process works; all that is required on the part of the gambler is the genuine commitment to change. Part One has been designed to give the reader an appreciation of the nature and extent of problem gambling before setting out on this program.

The principles and guidelines outlined in this book are based on clinical and research experience gained during more than twenty years of assisting problem gamblers. Most importantly, the techniques described in the book have been evaluated in long-term controlled treatment outcome studies carried out in a university setting to make sure that they really are effective. As a result, it is a practical book which teaches specific skills and behaviors to help you combat the urge to gamble and to correct the common irrational beliefs that foster persistence in betting and play.

This book gives the gambler direction in how to go about regaining control over behavior and guidance in pinpointing the goal, whether abstinence or controlled gambling. Equally important, it will be of help to many others who may be motivated to help the gambler. It gives information which will give family members an understanding of the difficulties surrounding the gambler in his/her attempts to cease. This will reduce confusion and guilt feelings, and help to dispel many myths and fears a spouse may have about the likelihood of cure and the future outcome. It gives advice on how to watch for tell-tale danger signs, on how to encourage those gamblers who refuse to face up to their problems to seek treatment, and on how to avoid the pitfalls that may make the problem worse. The book will also help employers to understand and assist workers whose jobs are threatened because of the detrimental influence of gambling on their performance.

The advice contained in this book can also be of benefit to gamblers for whom the activity has not yet reached problem level, especially adolescents or those early in their gambling career. The conviction that 'It won't happen to me' is so often wrong, as I have seen time and again when talking to young adult problem gamblers. I believe that prevention is better than cure. Therefore, part of this book is devoted to emphasizing that anyone, irrespective of income or intelligence, can be at risk, describing the process by which gambling may become a problem and highlighting how to detect the early warning signs.

This book takes no moral stance on gambling. It does not adopt the attitude that all gambling is wrong or immoral and should be banned. The Prohibition era in the 1920s showed very effectively that society cannot prevent gambling. Nor does it follow the Victorian view of the problem gambler as a weak personality lacking moral fibre. This could not be further from the truth. We recognize that most gamblers gamble sensibly and for fun. But for perhaps 1 per cent of gamblers, the urge to gamble and emotional dependence on gambling reach excessive levels and create problems for themselves and others. The cravings and drive to gamble are often as strong as those of the alcohol or drug addict. These are the people who need help, and to whom this guide is specifically directed.

PART ONE

About Problem Gambling

'Sweating on the Win'

My heart is pounding. I am standing on my toes, every muscle in my body tense as I watch the horses hurtling toward the finishing post. All I can think of is winning, winning just that amount of money that will let me draw even again. I just need this one piece of luck and I'll be free again. The last three races have cost me dearly, I'm down to my last few pounds and if I lose again, I know I'm in real trouble. Excitement, fear, panic – these are the emotions overwhelming me, all mixed in together, what a buzz. This is a real high. Look at them go, my horse is edging in front, I'm going to win, I know I am . . .

I had no intention of betting on the horses today. I'm sick of being behind all the time, borrowing money from friends for lunch, no money to take the kids out, the car needs repairs and Emma, my wife, wants to go on holiday this Easter. This has been going on for the last four years and at age twenty-seven, I should have at least some money to buy things for the family. Now was the time to be strong: I was determined without fail to pay this month's rent. Already two payments behind and some more bills to come, I kicked myself for betting last week when I already had the money. I should have known better. But then, when I read the form guide and saw that one horse I knew was a certainty running over its favourite distance and at those odds, I just had to grab the chance. A win of this size would solve all my problems. The thought of that win just wouldn't go away, running through my mind constantly. The urge to gamble was too great, nothing else mattered, I had to place that bet no matter what. No thought of the possibility that I could lose ever entered my head.

I felt bad about lying to my wife that I was called in to do some overtime. It was a bit risky, too, because she could ask for the money to buy Rachel the shoes she needed for school. But this was the only way to leave the house without suspicion. I'd kick myself if this horse won without me backing it. It happened before and I was really angry. I blamed Emma for making me go to that damn party. I would have been five hundred in front and not in this mess now. I'm not making the same mistake twice. Anyway, she'll be happy enough when I give her some of the winnings. What she doesn't know won't hurt her.

Gee, I hate that wave of numbness that comes on when you lose your last penny. That horse would have won if the damn jockey didn't pull it so early. His fault totally – but that doesn't make me feel any better. Look at what I've done: I'm behind again, I've lied to my wife, Rachel will miss out again. To make matters worse, what will I tell Emma about the supposed overtime pay? I know, I lent it to Peter, he had to pay some medical bills for his wife. No question that Emma will swallow that one.

This is getting out of hand. No more, I promise. I get nothing out of gambling except feeling miserable and down and I keep taking it out on the family. It's not fair, I should wake up to myself. No more, I promise for sure.

Yes!! The horse has won, I've done it ! I knew I would, no sweat. Gee, I feel great, on cloud nine! Three hundred pounds, what a beauty, I'm on a roll here. I can pay the bills now. But listen, I could double this three hundred on the next race. With six hundred the next few rent payments would be easy. I will win again, I'm positive. Yes, I'll go for it. If I start losing, I'll stop when I'm down to two hundred. I promise.

What is Gambling and When is it a Problem?

Atlantic City, early 1980s, Bally's Park Casino Hotel: the venue for my first international conference on gambling and risk-taking. It was also my first exposure to a casino. I hurried through hotel registration, deposited my luggage in my room, tipped the bellboy and with excited anticipation headed for the gambling floor. The cascade of noise, lights and movement of people all added to the dazzling atmosphere. Straight to the roulette table where I stood for several minutes watching others play and becoming familiar with the house rules. I took out the one hundred US dollars which I had set aside for gambling – the maximum I would allow myself to lose – and exchanged it for gambling chips. They were blue, I recall. The minimum stake was five dollars. Luck went my way, and after twenty minutes I was well in front. My urge satisfied, I left the table three hundred and sixty dollars richer. Tomorrow I would return and make more.

Early that next evening, I and several other delegates returned to the tables. Confident that my luck would con-tinue, I chose the same roulette table and began playing. No win came. What was wrong, I asked, had they changed the wheel, was the croupier spinning the wheel differently? Soon the winnings from the day before had disappeared. I was down to my last twenty dollars of the allocated gambling kitty. My heart was pounding as I watched that last spin. I had to win. It didn't happen. I felt a surge of anger. It was directed toward myself: why didn't I quit while I was in front? Now what would I do? I had lost not only my initial kitty but my winnings as well. I thought, 'I must draw out some more cash and try and win that money back. I'll stop once I win back the amount I lost, the amount that really belongs to me'.

I hastily retreated to the automatic bank teller machine conveniently located nearby, intent on taking out some of my holiday money to use to win my money back. But as I approached the machine I slowed down. Stop, I thought; I'm falling into the same pattern, the same trap, described by many of the gamblers I treat.

Let's deal with this situation sensibly, I said to myself. First, relax, slow down, reduce my level of arousal and feeling of agitation and pressure to obtain more money. Now, let's rethink the consequences of what I am doing. If I take my holiday money and lose that, how will I feel? Miserable and more angry at myself. And what will I do then? Take out more money to chase my losses? And if I lose that as well? Will I keep doing the same thing until I lose everything? If I have no money, then I will not be able to do what I had planned for my holidays. I will certainly be unhappy and remorseful.

I argued with myself. I could win, I insisted, my luck is bound to change.

Let's be realistic: gambling pushed me into this situation, more gambling won't get me out. My clients have taught me this through their own behavior.

But the money I lost is rightfully mine, I should try and get it back.

Rubbish: the money I spent was for entertainment. I bought some excitement and enjoyment from the casino operators. The money is not mine, it's theirs. They provided me with an opportunity for fun, playing roulette, in exchange for payment. This is much the same thing as when I pay the box office for a ticket to enjoy myself at the cinema. If the show is bad, I don't go back to the ticket office and ask for my money back, do I? I accept that my money is gone. The same principle applies to gambling.

So I decided to learn from my clients' behavior and avoid being trapped by the same pitfall. I relaxed and challenged my thoughts, considering the consequences of how I would feel when, not *if* but *when*, I lost again. Cut and accept my losses and do not create more problems; this was the proper approach.

It was not easy the next two days, watching others gamble and experiencing the urge to try my luck again. But applying what I had learnt about the process from my clients and the techniques described in this book, I resisted the impulse to return to the roulette. I lost my kitty as expected, but no more; and then, having returned home, went on to spend a most enjoyable few days holidaying in Hawaii.

With help from this book you can overcome your gambling compulsion and raise the overall quality of your life by improving your financial position, your relationships with others, and your ability to cope more effectively with pressure. The aim of this self-help guide is to help you regain control over your compulsive gambling habits by giving you a greater understanding of what gambling is and teaching you ways in which you can challenge and correct your distorted thoughts about gambling. It may not be easy, but remember: the results depend on the effort you put into helping yourself.

What is Gambling?

Gambling is an attractive form of entertainment which most people have enjoyed at one time or other in their adult life. In contemporary society, it is common for people to play cards for money with family members or school friends, bingo, fruit-machines and other forms of gaming machines; to purchase lottery or raffle tickets or enter sweepstakes; to bet off-track or visit casinos. All these activities are regarded as fun and are socially approved forms of leisure. Gambling in the company of friends, the possibility of winning and the gambling environment with its noise and lights all combine to make the experience attractive and exciting. Dreams of vast wealth and changes in fortune also entice people to try their luck: a jackpot could easily help pay off the mortgage, or mean an overseas holiday or a new car. However, most people are realistic: they hope to win, but really expect to lose. They only stake money that they can afford to lose.

Although there may be a sense of disappointment at having lost, there is no concern about it by either the gambler or family members. It is apparent that the physical arousal which is experienced as excitement is the main factor attracting people to gambling.

What exactly is gambling and how do we distinguish it from other risk-taking activities? Perhaps the most simple explanation of what gambling is has been given by two American psychologists involved in the treatment of problem gamblers, D. W. Bolen and W. H. Boyd. They described gambling as 'the wager of any type of item or possession of value upon a game or event of uncertain outcome in which chance, of variable degree, determines such an outcome'.

We can say that there is general agreement that there are at least five essential components included in gambling:

1 Two or more parties are involved (one can be an organization).
2 Events are based on uncertainty.
3 Items of value are redistributed according to the outcome of those uncertain events.
4 Items of value are not limited to money.
5 Participation is voluntary.

While the item of value that is staked is usually money, there have been cases in which people have bet possessions, property and even the sexual favours of their wives or daughters. According to one anecdote, a London police constable in the late 1800s chanced upon two shabbily dressed men in a quiet, foggy side street. One man was assisting the other, who appeared to the constable to be trying to hang himself from the lamp-post. When he attempted to intervene and save the man from what he thought was suicide, the constable was told in no uncertain terms to go away and mind his own business. It transpired that one of the men was so sure that he had the winning hand in a game of cards that he bet his life he would win. Unfortunately, he lost and was now in the process of paying his debt.

Specifically excluded from the definition are activities that involve some degree of risk but do not include the transfer of items of value. This extends to such risk-taking behavior as hang-gliding, crossing the road or driving fast – despite popular statements, for example, to the effect that 'the traffic is so heavy these days that it's a *gamble* trying to cross the road without being hit'.

Gambling in Society

There is nothing new about gambling, nor is it a peculiarly modern phenomenon. It is interesting to follow the development of gambling through the ages to shed some light on how society has reacted to problem gambling. Evidence exists to show that people have been gambling since ancient Egyptian times, 4000 years BC. Archaeological findings reveal that six-sided dice were used by the Etruscans and Romans around 900 BC and that in idle moments, Greek and Roman soldiers keenly wagered on the turn of numbered chariot wheels. This was the forerunner of roulette, a device refined by the French mathematician Blaise Pascal and introduced to England in 1739. It entered America in the nineteenth century and Australia as recently as 1973, where the game is now so popular that every Australian state and territory has one or more casinos.

Playing cards originated in twelfth-century China and reached Europe through Spain around the mid to late 1300s. Lotteries existed in early Roman days. Lots, that is, the casting of numbers, were used by early courts in determining guilt, dividing property and electing politicians. Lotteries became popular as a means of raising funds for public projects. Queen Elizabeth I introduced lotteries to England in 1569 to finance public projects and the support of the poor. Lotteries raised funds for the American War of Independence: George Washington is reputed to have purchased the first ticket. According to an article by the Chicago Crime Commissioner Virgil Peterson published in 1950, by 1790 'the lottery mania appear[ed] to rage with uncommon violence . . . Unscrupulous promoters incited the get rich mania among the people.' Horse racing, as John Day has noted, is 'a couple of thousand years older than Christianity'; Homer, Ovid and Herodotus were among the earliest of turf writers. Although public races were common in eleventh-century London, thoroughbred racing evolved from the horse-breeding interests of King Henry VIII (1509–47). The sport gained status as a national pastime under King James I (1603–25), was suppressed only temporarily during Oliver Cromwell's reign and came to be formally regulated following the establishment of the Newmarket Jockey Club in 1750.

The poker machine, also known as the fruit or slot machine, was invented by the American Charles Frey in 1895 and has gained popularity as one of the most profitable gambling devices ever invented; as one anonymous writer put it, 'No other machine was ever invented from which profits derived were so fabulous on so small an investment, and with so little effort.'

Sociological and anthropological studies have shown that gambling is a near-ubiquitous phenomenon, found in almost every race and culture throughout history. The only exceptions are a few Native American and Australian aboriginal societies in which wealth is owned in common rather than personally by individuals.

In western society, socio-political forces have brought about a major change in attitudes toward gambling since the early decades of the twentieth century. In 1931, Nevada permitted certain forms of gambling; now most states in the USA allow one or more forms. In England, the 1960 Betting and Gaming Act, which legalized off-course betting, ushered in a rise in gambling activity, a trend now clearly visible across Europe. Since the 1970s there has been unprecedented support for gambling as a legitimate form of community leisure activity, promoted by an extensive social, economic and political infrastructure.

The popularity of gambling is all the more interesting because of the absence of any obvious explanation of the drive to engage in this kind of behavior in the form of an underlying biological need or a substance which could be seen to produce a physiological response, as in alcohol or drug use. Heavy media promotion undoubtedly has an important influence on children and adolescents in encouraging them to see gambling as an exciting leisure activity. Advertising glamorizes gambling and lures people into it by giving the misleading impression that winning is a routine event and that most players come out as winners. While it is true to say that most people win on occasion, and that some of these wins may be large, the odds remain in favour of the house and invariably the vast majority of people lose in the long term. Studies have shown that most gamblers almost always return their winnings through further gambling. There is a tendency not to be satisfied with the amount won, to believe that more money can be gained by continued gambling.

Exactly how many people participate in some form of gambling is determined by the availability and accessibility of gambling facilities. The greater the availability of gambling outlets, the greater the number of people who participate. And the greater number of people who participate, the greater the number of those who are placed at risk of developing a problem – of becoming what are popularly known as 'compulsive gamblers'. As gambling becomes more popular and new forms are introduced, increasing concern is being expressed by welfare organizations and by mental health professionals who recognize and deal with its darker side, the personal, social and economic impact of problem gambling: for example, the failing health of the seventy-year-old who goes without food in order to have money to play the slot machines; or the pain of a family coping with the suicide of the father and the crisis of a ten-thousand-pound debt.

Before we look more closely at excessive and problem gambling, let us first pause and consider some of the terminology used to describe it, and some of the forms that gambling takes.

Terms Used to Describe Problem Gambling

To avoid confusion, it is important to differentiate the various terms commonly used of people who have lost control over their gambling behavior.

Most people are probably most familiar with the term 'compulsive' gambling through its association with Gamblers Anonymous – a self-help group for people who experience recurrent uncontrollable urges to gamble. However, uncontrolled gambling has also been referred to as 'excessive', 'addictive', 'dependent', 'neurotic' and 'pathological'. Although used interchangeably, these terms do have important differences from a scientific point of view. For example, the popular description 'compulsive' is not really accurate when we consider the specific psychiatric definition of the word. In psychiatry, a compulsion refers to a persistent urge to carry out a behavior that the person wishes to resist but is unable to because of high levels of anxiety and a fear that something bad will happen. It describes a condition known as obsessive-compulsive disorder in the broader class of anxiety disorders and is used to cover such behaviors as ritual hand-washing or repetitive checking. The person suffering the condition wishes to stop the behavior because it is irrational and causes distress.

This is not the case with 'compulsive' gamblers, who are, on the contrary, highly motivated to carry out their behavior. They gain immense subjective excitement and arousal from gambling. The pressure to stop often comes from outside sources, in particular from people around them who recognize the financial ruin and personal distress caused by patterns of excessive gambling behavior. This frequently puts the gambler in a position of conflict with those close to him or her. However, once you admit that gambling is causing problems either to yourself or to your loved ones, or both, then you are on the way to recovery.

In the early 1980s, largely through the efforts of the late Dr Robert Custer, an American psychiatrist, the term 'pathological gambling' came to be widely used in the field of mental health as the preferred description. 'Pathological' is a medical term suggesting the presence of an underlying disease process. Its use in this context implied that pathological gambling was in some way a mental illness or disorder, with many features suggesting its equivalence to an addiction.

This disease model has been severely criticized, particularly by John Rosencrance, a professor of criminal justice who was tragically injured in a motor vehicle accident in outback Australia after presenting a seminal paper at a gambling conference, on the grounds that it unjustifiably medicalized a social behavior. He and other clinicians have argued strongly that 'pathological' gambling is not a disease but a behavior that falls on a continuum ranging from social and intermittent at one end through regular and heavy to excessive at the other: there is no real difference between the merely heavy and the 'pathological' gambler except for the amounts gambled. As a result, to get away from the medical disease model, many health professionals now prefer the neutral description of 'problem' gambling.

All these terms have their limitations. However, for the purposes of this self-help book we will use 'pathological' and 'compulsive' gambling in an equivalent sense to describe gamblers who display clear signs of loss of control. 'Problem' gambling is used to refer to the wider group of people who show some but not all signs of developing that condition. In this book we will concentrate on the group of people who are commonly described as compulsive gamblers. It is true that some compulsive gamblers are in reality heavy gamblers who have temporarily lost control. This distinction does not, however, affect the applicability of the step-by-step self-help guide in Part Two of this book, which can be used equally effectively by compulsive, problem and heavy gamblers alike.

Before we turn to the clinical features of compulsive gambling and how it may be overcome, we should first look at what it is about certain types of gambling that means they are more likely to cause problems.

The Common Forms of Gambling

The mediums of gambling are almost limitless. People bet between themselves on the outcome of an event such as who will win the next football match, how many goals will be scored or who will score the first goal. These are informal agreements between participants with no set rules beyond those agreed to by them. In reality, the range of this type of gambling is limited only by the imagination of the players.

On a more formal level, organizations may operate certain games or activities within a framework of rules and regulations governing how the business will be conducted, often under national legislation or strict government guidelines which are imposed to minimize cheating and crime and to ensure fair play. Casinos and off-track betting are good examples of gambling systems run in this way.

Over the years many different activities have been regarded as 'gambling'. The list includes such pursuits as cards, dice, roulette and lotteries, as well as devices such as fruit or slot machines. You may be more surprised to learn that in the past even hobbies and sports such as tennis, walking and football were considered to be gambling mediums and were banned. Now, across the world organized betting takes place on the results of such disparate contests as elections and dog- and cock-fights, as well as on all major sporting events. Even promotional prizes offered by companies in pursuit of business and by retailers in shopping complexes constitute gambling.

Out of all this bewildering variety, four main categories of legal gambling can be identified: gaming, betting, lotteries and speculation.

- *Gaming* is the exchange of money on the outcome of a game. This category includes card games, fruit machines, video-draw poker machines, slot machines, two-up and casino games such as baccarat and roulette.
- *Betting* is staking money on the outcome of a future event. This category includes horse races (on the flat and over

jumps), greyhound races, other sporting events and elections.

- *Lotteries* are the distribution of money by 'lot' or number, and include instant 'scratch' cards, raffles and bingo as well as lotteries themselves.
- *Speculation* is gambling on business, insurance or stock markets.

You may be puzzled to think that business and financial investments can be regarded as gambling. Technically these meet the definition of gambling; but society has come to view them as falling within the bounds of economic activity. Many people now accept insurance as a means of protection and social security. Similarly with regard to business ventures and stock market trading (but excluding trading in commodity futures and some other financial instruments), it is argued that economic skills and sound business judgment are crucial elements brought to bear to minimize risk and maximize profits, and that far more than pure chance or luck is involved.

Which Forms of Gambling Cause Problems?

It should be clearly emphasized that not all forms of gambling lead to problems. Different levels of risk are associated with different types of gambling. Very few people experience impaired control over buying raffle tickets. There is a prolonged delay between the purchase of a ticket and its draw, and the draws are generally infrequent. On the other hand, many people suffer from fruit-machine, horse-race or lottery mania. Here, the delay between the 'purchase', that is, placing the bet, and knowing the outcome is very short, and the opportunity for further play is high; perhaps only a few seconds, several minutes or just a day or so.

It has been shown that those forms of gambling which readily lead to loss of control have two elements in common:

- the opportunity to place single large bets (as in horse-racing or casinos) up to several thousand pounds; and/or

15

- the opportunity to place frequent small bets over relatively short periods (as in fruit-machines), where the interval between play may be less than twenty seconds.

A further consideration is ease of access to gambling facilities. People are less likely impulsively to go to an off-course betting office if it is located several miles away. The inconvenience of travel and/or parking vehicles is sufficient to cause them to reconsider the strength of their urge. This is precisely the reason why casinos in some countries require twenty-four hours' notice of intent to gamble or are located in non-metropolitan areas: the delay imposed between the decision to gamble and gaining access to the facilities allows would-be gamblers a period in which the urge can dissipate and they can reconsider their intent.

When in Cairo recently, for example, I attempted to enter a casino for research purposes; but I was barred from entry until I could produce my passport. To get it, I had to return to my hotel. On entering the casino I discovered that all wagers had to be made in US dollars; local currency was prohibited. By this stage, any interest in playing roulette had disappeared, because I could not be bothered with exchanging foreign currency. This strategy was directed at, and highly effective in, protecting local residents from gambling.

Similarly, the wife of a patient recently complained bitterly that her husband had shown no interest in gambling until an off-track betting office opened within walking distance of their home. In the space of three months he had lost seven hundred pounds and had become irritable and distant, a changed personality. Despite her repeated protestations, he continued to gamble in the vain hope of recovering the amounts he had already lost. He had begun chasing losses.

Accessibility is important in terms of time as well as location. Facilities which are open from early morning until late at night can cater to a wider range of clients, including those working shifts as well as those with regular work hours.

Gambling in Excess

It has long been acknowledged that excessive gambling produces social and economic costs: poverty, starvation, family disintegration and criminal behavior. One of the first reported cases refers to an ancient Egyptian who was condemned to slavery in the salt mines for gambling to excess. Aristotle criticized gamblers, and the Jews debarred them from holding public office or appearing as witnesses because of their characteristic flaws and untrustworthiness. Religious attitudes varied, but some condemned gambling outright. The Qur'an forbade it, and eleventh-century Christian clergy were admonished for retarding the spread of the Church through their encouragement of gambling.

Gambling was not of itself illegal under English common law, but various Acts of Parliament were introduced to lessen breaches of peace and public order, corruption and cheating. Similar concerns are often expressed today about the relationship between gambling and organized crime, money laundering and cheating. Statutes of Richard II (1388), Edward IV (1477) and Henry VIII (1541) legislated against gambling in order to prevent impoverishment among soldiers, and to promote archery practice and military preparedness by eliminating the practice of gambling weapons.

In England and France alike, the negative impact of excessive gambling led to the government taking action to curb or restrict the practice. Severe penalties were imposed; for example, the criminal offence of vagrancy was extended to cover illegal gamblers who, for repeated offences, were branded, enslaved or executed. America responded to issues of family welfare, public safety and juvenile delinquency with the enactment of anti-gambling legislation in the mid-1700s.

Concerns similar to those expressed today by welfare organizations stemmed from the realization that the problem was widespread within the community. Severe loss and tragic consequences were common. Among the many famous historical figures who reputedly either manifested signs of excessive gambling or who had ruin brought upon them are Lord Halifax,

Lord Shaftesbury, Voltaire, Horace Walpole, Marie Antoinette and Nell Gwyn. The historian John Ashton in 1898 observed that the 'number of great men who played heavily, the number of fortunes wrecked at this time is almost incredible', and cited as illustrative examples the cases of Charles James Fox, Lord Carlisle and the Duke of Wellington, who had to sell his commission to clear his gambling debts. The same comment could be made today, with a number of sports figures, celebrities and leading business identities losing vast sums due to their gambling. A prominent lawyer in Australia was recently imprisoned for embezzling in excess of a million dollars from his trust funds to support his gambling.

The compulsion to gamble is well described by the historian Clemens France, who wrote in 1902 that many gamblers

> in their desperation strip themselves on the spot of their clothes, either to stake against money or to pledge the keeper of the table for a trifle to renew their play, and many instances occur of men going home half naked, having lost their all . . . The passion for gambling gives no time for breathing; it is an enemy which gives neither quarter nor truce; it is a persecutor, furious and indefatigable.

Consider the similarity of France's description with that of a letter written by a compulsive gambler in 1997:

> I have had gambling problems for the last nine years betting on horses. My gambling has caused me to appear before the courts on no less than four occasions. I have been homeless many times and my life has become unmanageable. When I am gambling, I do not think of the consequences, I don't care about anything else. I have readily blown my rent and food money to have that one more chance to win. It doesn't worry me. My second wife has left with the two children, both under three years of age. Even so, all I can dream of is the big win which will turn my life around for the better.

In 1817, lotteries were prolific but, according to France, the 'depression and excitement that so invariably followed the drawings diverted the labourer from his work, weakened his moral tone, consumed his earnings and soon brought pauperism'. By 1882 virtually every European state prohibited gambling.

Historically, the primary aim of anti-gambling legislation has been the social protection of community members. Certain activities, although inherently enjoyable in their own right, are seen to need restriction because of their deleterious effect and cost to the community as a whole. Yet people voluntarily pursue the opportunity to gamble, despite efforts to prevent them doing so, because most see gambling as an essentially exciting leisure pursuit and as offering a prospect of quick and easy wealth. Moreover, many governments see it as a lucrative source of revenue, and are consequently reluctant to limit it too far.

For some people, the urge to gamble is so persistent and excessive that it causes severe interference to many aspects of their own life, as well as to the lives of their spouses and family members. To gain a better understanding of the strong psychological forces acting upon you, the gambler, I recommend reading some of the descriptions contained in classical works of literature such as Pushkin's 'The Queen of Spades', Thackeray's 'A Gambler's Death', Saki's 'The Stake' and Dostoevsky's 'The Gambler'. Dostoevsky's description of the irresistible urge is based upon his personal experience, for he himself was, as P. Squires has described, 'powerless in the clutches of his terrific gambling mania, which blunted his sense of moral responsibility as effectively as extreme alcohol addiction could'.

We know that the majority of people who gamble to excess develop psychological symptoms of depression and anxiety; many turn to alcohol or drugs as a means of temporarily escaping their problems. But do not despair; the cycle can be broken and recovery achieved. In some cases, the stress of financial pressures may even be so strong as to lead the person to commit a crime in order to cover his debts or provide money with which to continue gambling. Yet even at this stage, appropriate action can be taken to reverse the situation and deal positively with problems. The fear of discovery and its repercussions strains the already fragile emotional state of the gambler, causing him or her to withdraw from social and family life; partnerships and marriage relationships deteriorate dramatically. The emotional turmoil interferes with concentration and the ability to perform properly at work, increasing the risk of being sacked. Yet again, with help, the partnership or marriage can be improved, and performance at work stabilized. In a large minority of cases, guilt and remorse coupled with agitation and fear of discovery and the concomitant intense public embarrassment and humiliation lead to serious suicide attempts. In such cases, proper care and management can be offered to reduce the likelihood of self-harm and, with support from those around, the process of recovery can be begun.

Remember: no matter how bleak the outlook appears, you can regain command of the situation and work toward personal development and self-improvement. Compulsive gambling is treatable and many do overcome its grip. This book is designed to be of assistance to this group of individuals in helping them regain control over their behavior and emotions and improve their quality of life, not to mention that of their families and those around them.

'I can remember exactly when my problem started. I was sixteen years of age. My friends and I managed to bluff our way into the bar for a few drinks. We started to play the fruit machines and after about half an hour I won what was a large amount of money to me, thirty dollars. I was so excited, my heart was racing and the fact that I had won made me feel so special. I thought, This is easy money. The next day I looked forward to returning to win more. I couldn't stop. Soon my friends were annoyed at my always wanting to go to the bar instead of the movies or to parties. I avoided them and gambled alone. Then once I lost more than I really could afford, I got angry; I had to win my money back. I kept going back. After a while my debts were so great that more gambling was the only way out. I became really depressed, but what angered me most was the lies I told to cover up what I was doing . . . But still I couldn't stop. The change came when I admitted my problem to my parents. They helped me to open up, to communicate with others and to deal with each problem I had created. They gave me hope. Through their efforts, my self-esteem and confidence grew. I owe them a lot.' John

What are the Characteristics of Problem Gambling?

Most people gamble sensibly within their financial means, but for a few, gambling is an over-riding passion that dominates many aspects of their life. They become obsessed with the anticipation of the next wager and preoccupied with thoughts of where to get more money so that they can carry on gambling. In these cases, the gambler is transformed into a withdrawn and moody person who is constantly plagued by worries about meeting debt repayments, finding daily living expenses and concealing debts.

These are the people for whom this book is written: those who are said to be compulsive gamblers. For them, the urge to gamble can no longer be controlled or managed, and as a result has a major impact on personal, family and work activities. Take Mary, a forty-five-year-old mother of two grown-up daughters. They have left home and she is on her own during the day, bored and lonely. Her advertising executive husband works late hours. She has developed a habit of going to bingo virtually every day; here she can forget about her hassles and disappear into a world of her own. The problem is that she is losing all her money, skimping on food and clothing purchases to have enough to go on playing. She has dreams of bingo almost every night and can hardly wait until her husband leaves for work in the morning so she can go to the bingo hall, where she spends most of the day. She neglects her appearance and the home, much to the confusion of her husband who is unaware of what she is doing.

The compulsion is so strong that it appears to be beyond

control. It may come on suddenly or after exposure to a particular cue or stimulus, for example, reading the lottery or race results in a newspaper. Once the thought of gambling enters the person's mind, it grows in strength to the extent that all concentration is directed toward finding ways of satisfying it as quickly as possible. In some instances, having begun gambling the person is totally possessed by the urge to the point where he or she may not be able to stop, even though they may need to return home or to work. The more the gambler is in debt and needs to win, the greater is the compulsion to return again and again.

Joanne is a 54-year-old housewife whose thoughts about playing the lottery have taken over her whole life. Every night she goes to sleep dreaming of winning the lottery, fantasizing how she would spend her money: pay off the kids' mortgages, travel to Barcelona, furnish her home the way she would like – new curtains, a new kitchen and carpets. She skimped on household spending just to get a few more pence for another ticket. It was a ritual each time a draw was to be televised. Each morning, she would wake excited almost unable to wait to watch the television; she would never go out just in case she missed the show. Her husband is fed up with her constant preoccupation with the lottery, her lack of interest in the marriage and their home, and the couple are now slowly drifting apart.

People who compulsively gamble to excess commonly report the following feelings.

Before gambling:

- An increasing preoccupation with gambling, to the point where nothing else is important. This is often experienced as sense of 'craving'.
- A fear that they may miss an opportunity to win. How many times have we heard of the unhappy person whose lucky numbers turned up but who had forgotten to buy their ticket?
- Irrational confidence and fantasies about winning.
- Excitement in anticipation of buying the 'winning' ticket. Fantasizing what to do with the winnings.

- Irritation, anger and mounting tension if something prevents them from gambling.

During gambling:

- A total focus of attention on gambling; all else fades in importance.
- Excitement and physical arousal, shown by increased heart rate.
- Irrational talk inside their head: the next bet is the winner I have been waiting for. It must be my turn soon for a large win, I just know it.
- Superstitious behavior to increase the chance of a win.

After a successful session:

- Relief and anticipation of the next occasion.
- Confidence (I knew I could do it) and a conviction that winning was a result of skill.
- Elated mood.
- Inflated ego, having beaten 'them' at their own game.
- Self-satisfaction at having money and being able to impress a partner or spouse.

After losing:

- Guilt and remorse.
- Fear of spouse or others finding out.
- Worry over where to obtain money to cover living expenses.
- Thoughts of what lies to tell to cover one's actions.
- Self-directed anger.
- Determination never to gamble again – but at the same time, thoughts of where to find money in order to return to chase losses.
- Desire to forget problems through alcohol.

One question often asked is whether there is a 'gambling-prone personality'. The answer is simple and straightforward:

there is *no* such gambling personality type. Furthermore, there is *no* individual personality trait that is commonly to be found in gamblers. Gamblers include all types of personality, and all kinds of personality traits are found in gamblers.

There are nevertheless general signs that partners and family members can look out for as signals that a problem might exist. These are:

- lengthy or unexplained times away from work and home;
- complaints of poor productivity at work;
- betting tickets suggesting large bets;
- preferring to play slot machines alone instead of remaining in social company at pub or club;
- always being short of cash despite regular income;
- having a number of credit cards with little available credit;
- having multiple loans;
- mood shifts coinciding with major race meeting days;
- preoccupation with studying the form guide, listening to races or watching race broadcasts;
- friends who comment on the amount of money borrowed from them;
- calls from creditors requesting payment for outstanding debts, or threats of legal action;
- sudden job changes;
- repeated bounced cheques;
- monies or items disappearing from the home;
- discovering less money in bank accounts than should be there.

For the individual gambler, a good self-assessment is obtained by answering honestly the twenty questions listed by Gamblers Anonymous. These are:

1 Did you ever lose time from work due to gambling?
2 Has gambling ever made your home life unhappy?
3 Did gambling affect your reputation?
4 Have you ever felt remorse after gambling?

5 Did you ever gamble to get money with which to pay debts or otherwise solve financial difficulties?
6 Did gambling cause a decrease in your ambition or efficiency?
7 After losing, did you feel you must return as soon as possible and win back your losses?
8 After a win, did you have a strong urge to return and win more?
9 Did you often gamble until your last dollar was gone?
10 Did you ever borrow to finance your gambling?
11 Have you ever sold any real or personal property to finance gambling?
12 Were you reluctant to use 'gambling money' for normal expenditures?
13 Did gambling make you careless of the welfare of your family?
14 Did you ever gamble longer than you had planned?
15 Have you ever gambled to escape worry or trouble?
16 Have you ever committed, or considered committing, an illegal act to finance gambling?
17 Did gambling cause you to have difficulty in sleeping?
18 Do arguments, disappointments or frustrations create within you an urge to gamble?
19 Did you ever have an urge to celebrate any good fortune by a few hours of gambling?
20 Have you ever considered self-destruction as a result of your gambling?

Some of the best predictors of pathological gambling are:

- the compulsion to chase losses;
- repeated failed efforts to stop gambling; and
- gambling in response to negative emotions such as stress and depression.

Despite the fact that gambling has led to the development of serious financial problems, compulsive gamblers hold a firm but wrong belief that more gambling is the solution to their troubles, that a win will save them by allowing them to pay off the debt. However, the cycle can be broken. With the help of this book, you can learn to identify the errors in your thinking. Once you understand the various steps down the path to problem gambling, you can reverse the process and change your behavior for the better.

2

How Does the Problem Develop?

Most gamesters begin at small games; and, by degrees, if their money or estates hold out, they rise to great sums; some have played first all their money, then their rings, coach or horses, even their wearing clothes and perukes; and then such a farm; and, at last, perhaps a lordship. (From *The Nicker Nicked*, published in 1619)

Usually, problems generated by gambling emerge gradually over a period of time. Many people are unable to recognize the exact point at which they lost control. All they are aware of is a steady progressive worsening of their financial situation and finding themselves needing to spend more time and money gambling and lying to others to cover up their behavior. Like many alcoholics, they do not see the problem for what it is until they are right in the middle of a crisis and when others complain about their actions. Even then, many will deny that there is anything wrong and react with anger and resentment at any suggestion that there is a problem. These people are in denial. Distortions in their thinking enable them to minimize the depth of their predicament or rationalize away their behavior, saying that this is only a temporary situation caused by some bad luck. They firmly hold the expectation that improvement is just around the corner.

The process leading to compulsive gambling is simple, but the pattern varies. Initially, people gamble at acceptable levels of expenditure, that is, only risking amounts that they can afford. However, at some point in time and often for reasons which are not entirely clear, control is lost. The loss of control may take one of two forms: an inability to resist an opportunity to gamble, or an inability to cease gambling once it has started.

> 'Looking back on it, I don't really know when it became a problem. All I know is that I found myself drawn back to the machines. I couldn't stop thinking about them. They had a magic that enchanted me and I spent more and more time playing. Gradually all my money, I mean *all* my money, was used to play those wretched machines. I felt really angry having to pay bills because it meant I had less to play with.'
> Mary

Loss of control may happen rapidly, the excitement of winning on the first few occasions being so profound that the person becomes addicted almost instantaneously. Early wins are also important in setting up the false expectations that one can make 'easy' money through gambling.

In other cases, the decline is gradual but progressive. Some individuals find that after many years of controlled behavior, the frequency and intensity of their gambling increase. They may sometimes gamble for longer and lose more money than they intended. Then, in the hope of making good their losses, they return to try their luck again, aiming to win to break even. This is the first step into the 'chasing cycle', a process well described by the American sociologist Professor Henry Lesieur in his book *The Chase*. The more gamblers try to recoup their losses, says Lesieur, the deeper they plunge into debt and the more pressure is exerted on them to return to repeat the cycle. So it goes on until they find themselves in a hopeless financial position.

Finally, as in alcoholism, some go on to gamble in binges. A binge is a sudden prolonged session or bout of excessive gambling. The main feature is a burst of frenetic gambling coupled with a subjective sense of impaired control where the person feels he or she just cannot stop. No consideration is given to what the final outcome will be. There is a sense of desperation and self-destructiveness as the gambler loses vast amounts over relatively short periods. The interval between sessions may vary in length from several weeks to many months, and is characterized by periods of remorse and minimal or no urge to gamble.

The Phases of Pathological Gambling

Clinicians have identified three phases through which most pathological gamblers pass in their career, although how quickly they pass through each phase, as I have mentioned, varies substantially. These are:

- the winning phase;
- the losing phase;
- the desperation phase.

The Winning Phase

We all have to start somewhere. In the winning phase, a person is introduced to some form of gambling, quite often by parents or friends. The idea is to have fun, so one quickly learns that gambling is associated with action and excitement. This excitement might be produced by the thrill of winning, enjoying some aspect of the gambling environment in the company of friends, or forgetting life's daily hassles and problems, at least for a little while. About three-quarters of compulsive gamblers report that they had a 'large' win some time shortly after they first began. The win does not have to be large in absolute terms, only in relation to one's income. To a twelve-year-old, a ten-pound win may represent a large amount. John was a boy of fourteen when his father gave him a scratch card. He remembers slowly scratching the card to reveal the right numbers to win two pounds. He wanted another, and soon another. It is worth remembering that the average age at which a person starts to gamble is around twelve to fifteen years of age; and it is usually parents, grandparents or friends who introduce an adolescent to gambling.

Winning leads to fantasies about winning more and an attitude that gambling is an easy and quick way of 'earning' additional income. Early wins, the 'beginner's luck' – perhaps more appropriately called 'beginner's *bad* luck' for some – give the novice gambler a sense of undue confidence in the ability to win and a strong belief in continued luck.

The Losing Phase

Unfortunately, we all know that luck does not hold out. The longer one gambles, the greater is the likelihood of losing. How many times have we heard someone complain that they won several pounds the first time they tried gambling but since then, they have lost it all and more besides. Peter, an electrician, was ecstatic when he won two hundred pounds on the slot machines during a work Christmas party at the club. He was the centre of attention, all his mates were talking about his luck. He felt good. He just had to return to play some more. He persuaded his friends to come with him because he wanted to impress them with his luck again. His ego-trip gave way to disappointment when he lost half his original winnings. Embarrassed and angry at himself, he went back by himself now, just to recover the amount lost. But he kept losing.

Eventually one loses more than one intends or can afford, and then attempts to recover by 'chasing' losses, that is, pouring more and more money into gambling with the hope of winning amounts already lost, as Peter had done. The unpredictability of the outcome, with wins coming every so often, reinforces this hope and encourages the chasing process. But repeated losses pull the gambler further and further behind and into debt, until he is prepared to take even greater risks in an increasingly desperate pursuit of the big win that will get him back to square one. The gambler begins secretive gambling, seeking sources of more money to gamble with, covering up losses and lying, losing time from work, borrowing from financial institutions, neglecting home life and failing to pay debts.

The Desperation Phase

Soon the gambler is plunged into the desperation phase, caught up in a cycle of chasing losses, winning occasionally, then suffering more losses and so on in a tightening downward spiral. Irrational gambling begins. The frequency and size of bets increase and bigger debts are accumulated until rock bottom is reached. Everything else is neglected – work, family relationships and social life. At this point the gambler is out of control. Nothing matters except finding more money to gamble, even to the point where many will begin to steal or embezzle funds to support their habit.

Lee, an ambitious 22-year-old bank teller, was given a tip by a customer for a good bet on an upcoming horse race. Lee was impressed because this customer frequently deposited large amounts, claiming that they were betting wins. He withdrew a hundred pounds from one of his customers' accounts, with the intention of using this to place his bet and returning it first thing in the morning before anyone could trace the transaction. He won. But then he repeated the process a few more times after being given further tips by his customer. Then came the fateful day when he lost heavily. He did not have enough money the following morning to cover up his transaction. So he carried out a transfer of funds from another account. The following day he lost again. Now he was transferring funds across two separate customer accounts. At this point, he should have recognized the danger signals and taken steps to discuss the matter with his wife and manager. It was still possible to minimize the damage. But he failed to act sensibly. Within twelve months he was seventy thousand pounds in debt, all of it embezzled from customers' accounts. Each morning he would be the first to arrive at work, feverishly transferring funds in an ever-increasing chain to avoid detection. After the stress of work he would go to the local bar each afternoon and drink to seek relief.

How was his deception discovered? His manager insisted that he take his annual leave. He refused, but to no avail. He knew what would happen. On the very first day of his absence, the replacement teller noted a discrepancy in one account of fifty pounds and informed the manager. The auditors were called, and by the week's end, Lee was facing a charge of fraud. The magistrate, recognizing his compulsive gambling habit, imposed a four-year jail term. His wife, left with a one-year-old daughter, was shattered. He had some luck left, though: his wife is supportive and is prepared to wait for his release.

Lee's is not an isolated case. Studies have shown that 60 per cent of compulsive gamblers commit a non-violent property crime such as theft, passing dud cheques, shoplifting, embezzlement or misappropriating company funds. In about 20 per cent of these cases, the gambler is caught and charged, sometimes incurring a sentence of imprisonment. For example, one legal secretary regularly took small amounts out of her petty cash system to play the slot machines during her lunch break. She became panicky when she was about one hundred pounds behind, and tried to win the money back by spending more time at the machines. Eventually she accumulated a loss of three thousand pounds. She could not afford to repay this amount from her weekly salary, so her only option seemed to be to continue gambling so that she could win enough to replace her losses and escape detection. Eighteen months later, a routine company audit uncovered a shortfall of eleven thousand pounds. She was charged, convicted and sentenced to six months in prison. Her husband and eight-year-old daughter were devastated.

These, admittedly, are among the more serious cases; but most gamblers commit acts that make them feel miserable within themselves, for example, stealing small amounts from a spouse or partner, or from the purse or wallets of friends, stealing items from work or forging signatures on cheques.

For people early on in their compulsive gambling career, this self-help book can prevent the decline into the desperation phase, while for those already there, it provides an effective strategy to begin the process of recovery.

3

Who is at Risk of Being Affected?

Many people gamble, but only a relatively small percentage lose control and suffer problems as a result. Therefore, it seems that not every one is at risk of developing compulsive gambling habits. Research has established some general guidelines for use in highlighting those individuals who may be particularly at risk. In this chapter we shall consider some of the more clearly identified factors that contribute to a high risk, before going on to set out three major paths of entry into problem gambling.

Risk Factors

Income is an obvious and important starting point. Findings have consistently shown that people on low incomes and unemployed persons are vulnerable to gambling problems. Low earners have less disposable income available to spend on leisure pursuits than those who earn high salaries. As a result, problems emerge at a much earlier stage in proceedings and tend to persist over a longer period, because of the wage-earner's limited resources and restricted access to financial assistance. For example, consider two individuals, one with fifty pounds disposable income a fortnight and the other with two hundred pounds. Assume both spend twenty pounds gambling. For one, this represents 40 per cent of his income; for the other, 10 per cent. Should both establish a debt of five hundred pounds and begin to pay it back at the same rate of forty pounds a week, the person on the lower income will struggle to meet the repayments, thus immediately facing the temptation to gamble more in order to try to ease the financial pressure. In addition, the person on the lower income is likely to find it much more difficult to borrow funds. In these circumstances, there is a greater risk of the person turning to illegal means to obtain money to supplement living expenses.

Age, gender and gambling medium are other risk factors which interact with one another. Young males between the ages of sixteen and thirty playing fruit and slot machines and betting on horse races are more at risk than their contemporaries purchasing weekly lottery tickets. Bingo and instant scratch cards have greater appeal for older females. There is some anecdotal evidence, according to David Miers, professor of law at Cardiff Law School, that scratch cards are more popular with working-class females, for whom betting in off-course betting offices is socially difficult, and mothers caring for children, who can easily purchase tickets during shopping trips.

The feature perhaps most consistently associated with problem gambling is impulsivity. Problem gamblers manifesting impulsivity show a tendency to have commenced gambling at an earlier age, spend more money gambling and display greater levels of financial difficulty than non-impulsive gamblers. They also show greater disturbances in other areas of their life: unstable work histories, poor interpersonal relationships and substance abuse.

As mentioned already, there is no known personality profile associated with an increased risk of impaired control over gambling. A number of studies have suggested that gamblers recorded higher scores on psychometric measures of depression, poor tolerance for boredom, addiction and anti-social personality, but it remains unclear whether these contribute to loss of control or are the end result of stress caused by the need to deal with problems generated by gambling. Nor is there any link between 'sensation-seeking' and gambling. On the contrary, studies have repeatedly shown that problem gamblers as a group achieved lower scores on such measures than members of the general population.

Perhaps the best way of seeing who is at risk is to look at the various pathways leading to the development of problem gambling.

An Integrated Model of Problem Gambling

There is a growing recognition that problem gambling is not a unitary disorder but affects several subtypes of people who share several features in common. I have proposed an integrated model which postulates three major entry pathways into problem gambling. Let us examine these in detail, because this will enable us to appreciate the multiple factors that act in combination to produce impaired control in gamblers.

Pathway One: The 'Normal' Problem Gambler

This first pathway is linked to the environment and learning. Environment is important in providing both the opportunity to gamble in the first place, and the advertising which glamorizes and actively promotes participation. Early large wins, intermittent winning and the excitement of the gambling environment combine to establish a gambling habit. At the same time, specific beliefs and attitudes are firmly set down; these include the notion that winning is possible, that one has above average skills or is able to influence the outcome during play, that luck is with or will soon come to one, and a tendency to dismiss losses in preference to concentrating on wins.

At some point, more money than originally intended is lost and the gambler begins to chase losses through further gambling. A habit emerges which is difficult to break, its continuance constantly encouraged by financial pressures.

People in this group do not necessarily have pre-existing psychological problems. Although they may show symptoms of depression, anxiety and substance abuse, these are emotional reactions which are secondary to the problems generated by gambling. Entry down this path may occur at any age in either gender, and may be triggered by exposure to gambling through the influence of chance, family members or friends. The intensity of gambling and the severity of the problems produced are lower for these gamblers than for those in the other groups. These gamblers have more insight into their problems, are more motivated to seek treatment of their own accord, are more likely to comply with treatment instructions and respond much better in terms of outcome. Individuals in this category are more likely to be able to resume controlled levels of gambling after treatment. If you are in this category, with the help of this book you have a very good chance of recovery.

Pathway Two: The Psychologically Vulnerable Gambler

Some people have difficulty managing stress or dealing with crisis situations. They may suffer from depression or anxiety and use methods which allow them to escape problems rather than confronting them directly. Lack of ability to cope with stress and deal with problems may have been caused by past traumas, child abuse, disturbed family upbringing or inadequate role models. These individuals may be suffering feelings of insecurity, low self-esteem and a sense of rejection. They develop feelings of personal unhappiness, low mood, anxiety and tension. For them gambling becomes a means of emotional escapism, a means by which they can forget their problems through the distraction of excitement.

Often in these circumstances, dissociation occurs. Dissociation is an alteration and distortion in perception which allows a person to split off and forget unpleasant emotions. A good example of dissociation in everyday experience is that of driving. You can no doubt recall a time when you were so preoccupied with thoughts that you may have driven several miles without being consciously aware of what you were doing. You were driving safely, only you didn't register your actions in consciousness. It was an automatic habit that you carried out. Similarly, in one case I saw recently, Allan would spend three or four hours playing the slot machines; but he could not remember how he got to the club or what he was doing during all that time. He said that he could remember suddenly being at the club, heading toward the machines, and then nothing until he was leaving the premises. His sense of time perception was dramatically altered; he would swear that he only spent less than half an hour gambling.

In this category we can identify a number of subgroups of gamblers, all in some circumstance of personal stress. We have the young male whose life ambitions are being frustrated. He has not achieved his ambitions at work; he sees his friends getting further and further in front of him in respect of marriage and advancement at work, and enjoying the benefits of a home, car and holidays. The gambler feels left behind, resentful and disillusioned. Problems at work are often taken home, creating family and partnership conflicts. In response and to escape home and work stress, the gambler finds satisfaction in gambling.

For some women, the stress of an unhappy relationship, disappointments, a failing marriage, loneliness or boredom with their life is sufficient to tip the balance over toward excessive gambling. They avoid succumbing to depression by immersing themselves in gambling. They see little future for themselves, trapped in unhappy circumstances from which they see no prospect of escape. Women tend to gamble at a later age in life than males, around forty to fifty. In a handful of cases, I have noted that women in conflict with their husbands, or who discover their husbands having affairs, will gamble excessively in an unconscious act of aggression directed at 'getting even' with their husbands by spending all their savings. Fortunately, women show a more positive attitude toward treatment and seek help much earlier than males.

For gamblers who are vulnerable, any stress, no matter what its source, can be sufficient to push them over the edge into compulsive gambling. Even positive events can have this effect. Several gamblers have said that they have gone on a gambling binge following the birth of a baby. Whether they felt rejected, reacted against all the attention being directed toward the baby, or were fearful of losing their wife's affection is uncertain; what we do know is that they have embarked on a chaotic episode of severe gambling over a short period.

If you find yourself in any one of these categories, be aware that your gambling will show a tendency to escalate during periods of stress or crisis. For you, abstinence is perhaps the best goal of treatment. In addition to the approaches described in this book, the techniques outlined in the self-help book in this series on dealing with panic and anxiety, *Overcoming Anxiety* by Helen Kennerley, will be very useful in helping you cope with stress and its effects on gambling.

Pathway Three: The Impulsive Gambler

There is a small group of gamblers who show signs of a wide range of impulsive behaviors from early childhood onwards. These people have often had problems with learning, concentration and attention at school; they find themselves being overactive and needing a lot of stimulation, becoming bored very easily, and like to get involved in new activities; they tend to do things on impulse without thinking about the consequences of their actions. They are more likely to experiment with alcohol and drugs from an early age, and to have difficulty holding down a job for any length of time because they lose interest in what they are doing; they generally do not have any long-term commitment or ambition in life. For these people, gambling starts at a much earlier age in childhood and can lead rapidly to serious financial trouble. Quite often the gambling occurs in binges, with the additional danger that they also become very depressed and begin drinking to excess, also in binges. This combination increases the risk of self-harm.

Peter was an intelligent 25-year-old spray painter who managed to get through school without doing much work. He was constantly in trouble for acting silly in class, much preferring to be out and about – he was involved in many different active sports – and as an adolescent was always in the thick of things, down at the clubs and bars or driving around on his motorcycle, frequently drinking too much and experimenting with a wide variety of soft drugs. From an early age he used to like betting on anything, even on a dare. He was never interested in hard work. He managed to find jobs easily because of his outward nature, pleasant personality and intelligence, but would never stay in one for more than six to twelve months. Once he was familiar with his work, he became bored and restless, and then turned to gambling and socializing instead. In his early twenties, he became more and more dissatisfied and depressed because he did not seem to be getting on in life. Fortunately, his girlfriend encouraged him to see a counsellor who taught him some of the techniques outlined in this book to help him control his impulsive behavior. Although he still breaks out occasionally, he is doing well after two years of counselling.

If you do happen to fall in this category of impulsive gamblers, then in addition to reading this book, it is important for you to obtain additional counselling and support from a clinical psychologist in your community health service, and also to contact a psychiatrist or family doctor who can prescribe some anti-depressant medication that may be of help to you.

4

What is the Effect of Problem Gambling on the Gambler?

Mr A.B. is a 25-year-old married electrical technician who began gambling on horses when he was eighteen. He attended one race meeting with several friends and won a reasonable amount of money from a small bet. This excited him and led him to believe that he had particular skills in picking winners. He then became a regular punter, placing bets through the off-course tote system. He enjoyed discussing the races with his workmates and studying the form guide.

Within twelve months he preferred to place bets by himself because this increased his opportunities to gamble. He began to gamble almost daily, frequently taking time off work to do so. Losses did not worry him excessively because he could borrow money, go without or pawn possessions.

He married at age twenty-two. Although aware that he bet on horses, his wife did not realize the full extent of his gambling behavior; and Mr A.B. was concerned that if she did, he would be forced to stop. Consequently, he concealed any evidence of his gambling. To cover up his losses, he opened secret bank and credit card accounts and started to juggle payments between the various accounts. This went on successfully for some time; however, eventually repeated losses meant that he had to take out loans. The debts mounted as he increased the size of each bet in the hope of winning enough to bail himself out.

His physical and emotional health started to deteriorate as a result of his constant preoccupation with his financial problems. He became moody and irritable and would often engineer arguments as an excuse to leave the house in order to place bets. These changes in his behavior put stress on his relationship with his wife.

Soon he had exhausted all legitimate sources of borrowing and began to steal items from work to sell in order to obtain cash. In the meantime, his wife was becoming worried about the changes in his personality. Because of his absences from work and the increasing amount of time he was away from home, she came to the conclusion that he was having an affair.

Eventually his illegal activities were detected and the police called in to investigate. His wife was horrified, both by his being charged over the offences and the need to appear before the courts, and by the huge debt that he had incurred. There was a risk that the couple would have to sell the family home in order to repay it all and also cover their legal costs. Her trust in her husband was completely undermined and she was considering leaving him.

The case history of Peter suggests several of the ways in which the pathological gambler will experience personal distress as a result of his or her overall predicament. The effects impinge on emotions, behaviors, physical health and thought processes. Some examples of these effects will be discussed below.

Depression

'I felt hopeless. Work no longer gave me any satisfaction. Nothing would perk me up, not even going to the cinema. Three thousand pounds in debt, I couldn't concentrate on meeting clients and selling the company products. I was wanting to read the form guide to select a winner in the next race, so I would cancel appointments or sell less just to get out of the meeting to listen to the race. My boss was on my back all the time and my wife needed a new washing machine. How was I to meet all these demands? Why can't people just leave me alone, I thought; all I want is to be left by myself. It got to the point where I no longer had the energy or the desire to put any effort into things. If only I could just lie in bed all day.'

Clinical research has consistently revealed that up to 75 per cent of compulsive gamblers suffer from symptoms of major depression. The symptoms of depression are low mood, feeling 'blue', withdrawal from others, loss of appetite, no interest in activities, poor motivation, sleep disturbance and irritability. Physical symptoms often include headaches and a general sense of feeling poorly. For the depressed person the future seems to be very bleak indeed, as one cannot see any solution or escape out of the pit of unhappiness.

Some clinicians suggest that depression is one of the driving forces leading people to gamble compulsively in the first place, while others suggest that it is the logical consequence of deep financial and personal trouble. This issue is yet to be resolved. What is clear is that unhappiness, loneliness and feeling poorly about yourself are hallmarks of the compulsive gambler; but they are hallmarks that can be removed.

Natalie gambled away her pension on the slot machines. She was five hundred pounds in debt on credit cards, was worried about her brother in a nursing home and upset over her daughter who was taking drugs. Living alone, she felt trapped in her situation, unable to see herself repaying her debts and being able to afford to live. For her, gambling was the only source of comfort and enjoyment in an otherwise empty life. Every night she would cry herself to sleep with worry.

In treatment, she was advised to seek assistance from a financial counsellor, who contacted her bank and arranged payments she could afford. Arrangements were also made for direct payments out of her pension to support her brother so that she did not have to worry or feel guilty that she was letting him down. Once help was being given to her daughter too, Natalie's mood started to improve and for the first time in a long while she began to look after her appearance, join in with other senior citizens on outings and feel better within herself. She says that she now cannot understand what she found in the slot machines and feels ill at any thought of going back to play them.

Suicidal Thoughts

It is not surprising that many gamblers are highly distressed and panicky about their financial problems and the fear of being discovered by their spouse, employer or the police if they have committed any offence. The inability to see a solution, coupled with the low mood of depression, results in a sense of hope-lessness, isolation and despair, while the deception and moodiness that go with pathological gambling put great strain on interpersonal relationships. This adds the fear that a partner or spouse will walk out, and anger and blame are directed toward oneself, weakening self-esteem. Alcohol abuse can exacerbate these feelings, which may eventually lead to suicidal ideas.

Let me illustrate the depth of the despair and poor judgment that can have tragic consequences for a few gamblers by citing from the transcript of a coroner's report into the death of a 32-year-old married man, found by his distraught wife hanging in the garage at his premises at about 11.50 a.m. on 20 September 1995. His wife confirmed to the police that over the preceding nine months he had lost a considerable amount of money at the casino: thirteen thousand pounds in all, in three lots of two thousand, four thousand and seven thousand pounds. After each loss he promised he would never return. Arguments over finances were becoming increasingly common, and his wife had to take out a further loan of six thousand pounds to pay off a credit card.

On the night of 4 September, he withdrew five hundred pounds from the automatic teller machine at the casino. He was back the following night, stating to a friend that he wished to recoup his losses. During that night he lost one thousand pounds, and a friend described him as distressed. On 11 September he took the day off work and went to the casino, where he withdrew two hundred and fifty pounds. A similar pattern occurred on 15 September involving a larger amount of seven hundred and fifty pounds. All the monies were taken from his joint account, in which only seven pounds now remained. In a state of depression on the final evening, he consumed a large part of a 750 ml bottle of whisky and left a brief note stating that suicide was the only means by which he could escape his debts and marital problems. The coroner concluded: 'The deceased was known to be suffering from depression due to financial difficulties resulting from gambling at the casino, and the gradual breakdown of his marriage relationship.'

This is not an unusual case. Up to 60 per cent of compulsive gamblers think about suicide at some stage during a crisis, and around 20 per cent have taken steps to make actual suicidal attempts. The true rate of suicide among pathological gamblers is not known, because generally coroners and doctors attribute the cause of suicide to depression without recognizing the crucial role that gambling may have played in causing the depression. As a result these deaths are not identified in the statistics of gambling-related suicides.

The risk of suicide is heightened if the person has a coexisting alcohol or drug problem or a family history of depression, or has committed serious criminal offences. In these circumstances, special attention should be given to offering as much support and encouragement as possible. Support from mental health professionals is strongly recommended in situations where suicidal thoughts or gestures have arisen. Blame and criticism do nothing more than aggravate the situation, so friends and family should be supportive.

Anxiety and Anger

'I explode at the drop of a hat. My kids avoid me; they're too scared to ask me to help with their homework because I yell at them. I just can't relax. Television just drives me batty, commercials and stupid shows. Yet I don't know what I want. I know I should be calmer and relate to my family but they don't understand. All they want is money for things, constant demands. I can't be expected to give them everything they want, can I? What about my needs? Don't I have a right to enjoy myself? What's wrong with a few bets?'

It is not surprising that the stresses associated with compulsive gambling produce high states of anxiety and tension. These are expressed in feelings of agitation, excessive worry over the future, muscular tension and the inability to relax. Muscular tension is also often expressed in physical symptoms such as headaches, back pains and general feelings of fatigue and tiredness.

Sleep is disturbed because of the constant worry and agitation. The lack of sleep causes fatigue, compounding the irritability and poor tolerance of frustration. Many partners of gamblers complain that the gambler's mood fluctuates dramatically in response to trivial events or for no easily understood reason. In a small number of cases episodes of panic attacks may occur. These are brief periods of intense anxiety during which a person is convinced that he/she will die or lose sanity.

With tension and anxiety come short temper, irritability and outbursts of anger. There are reports that 15–20 per cent of pathological gamblers express some anger toward family members and may even physically or verbally abuse their spouses and children. Many of the people I have treated say that they deliberately engineer arguments in order to have an excuse to get out of the house to gamble. This also provides an opportunity for them to turn the argument around and place blame on the partner for causing tension which 'forces' them to go off and gamble. 'If only she trusted me more, but she doesn't. If she thinks I'm gambling, damn it, I might as well do it, be hung for a sheep not a lamb' – these are words I often hear from clients. In a few instances, a man has hit his wife just to intimidate her so that she will think twice about questioning him over his behavior and to get what he wants: money, time to gamble, and silence. Many gamblers intimidate their spouses or partners to avoid social embarrassment by making sure that no one finds out about their gambling.

One of the main benefits offered by this self-help book is the relaxation technique it describes: while it is aimed primarily at controlling the gambling, it is reported by many gamblers to be helpful in calming their anxiety and anger in general. They say that once they have grasped this technique, they no longer become easily angered but stay in control much more easily than before.

Alcohol Consumption

'I started to drink at first because it helped me to forget about the money I lost at the machines. I used to feel dreadful when I lost all my money. I thought, what will my wife say? I just didn't want to go home and face her.'

Many people use alcohol and drugs to escape their worries and to overcome their feelings of anxiety or low self-confidence. It comes as no surprise to find that there is a high rate of coexisting alcohol- and drug-related problems in pathological gamblers. Studies have shown that between 20 per cent and 40 per cent of pathological gamblers exhibit symptoms of alcoholism while a smaller number, around 4–10 per cent, use illicit drugs. If you do drink excessively, then it is more likely that your gambling will be out of control and result in more severe problems. Remember, one of the effects of alcohol is to impair your judgment and make you feel overconfident in your own ability to win. You are more likely to take greater risks and to risk more money than you would otherwise.

Alcohol also affects self-control and interferes with your ability to avoid temptation or to stop gambling once started. Sometimes, excessive alcohol consumption causes a person to go on a single binge episode where a large amount of money is lost. The effect of this is devastating: the person starts to panic, drinks more in response to worry and then begins to borrow money to continue gambling to try and recoup losses. Recognizing the signals and knowing how to respond under these circumstances is essential to minimize the harm. The section later in this book on how to stop chasing losses (Step 5 in Part Two) is particularly relevant here.

Alternatively, a person may lose excessive amounts of money during an individual gambling session, become depressed and then turn to alcohol to deaden the emotional and mental pain.

Those persons more at risk of developing alcohol and drug

46

problems are those who have a family history of alcoholism, are suffering depression and anxiety, or exhibit signs of an anti-social personality, that is, a personality style characterized by disregard for social rules and conventions.

It is important to try and recognize within yourself what the main problem is. Is it the alcohol, the gambling or a combination of both? In other words, the question should be asked: is this a gambler who has an alcohol problem as a result of excessive gambling, or is this an alcoholic whose alcoholism leads him/her to lose control over gambling? This question must be addressed in order to gain a proper understanding of these disorders and an appropriate approach to their management. Attention must be given to teaching control over both forms of behavior, otherwise one behavior will act as a trigger for the other. The risk is that gambling will trigger an alcoholic to resume drinking because of the stress and depression associated with losing. Similarly, use of alcohol will trigger a gambling episode once the person is exposed to gambling cues.

One adolescent who was starting to do extremely well in treatment said that no one had picked up on the fact that he often spent time with his friends at the local bar. He would go with his friends and limit his drinking because he was the only one with a driver's licence. When his best friend obtained his licence, he felt that he could now drink more than his usual amount. On the second occasion, he felt confident in himself that he could control his gambling and thought that he should put himself to the test. He did well that time, so he thought he could continue – but promised himself that he would not go overboard. On the fourth occasion, he drank too much and began taking more risks. Predictably, he lost, felt that he had returned to square one and, in despair and anger at himself, gave up and started to binge in a self-destructive way. The whole process could have been halted if only he had learnt some of the simple strategies for relapse prevention outlined in this self-help book.

Employment

'I couldn't concentrate on work. Every half hour I would go to the toilet, sit down and be glued to my portable radio listening to the race broadcast. My boss finally suggested I see a doctor about my frequent need to use the toilet because he was worried about my health!'

An exceedingly high proportion of gamblers report that their gambling has in some way interfered with their ability to perform effectively in their jobs. This interference with work takes the form of reduced productivity, absenteeism, poor concentration and attention, lost opportunities for promotion, failure to follow up potential sales or new clients, and not showing initiative. Also, constant attempts to borrow from colleagues and failure to repay debts, and the desire to conceal the level of gambling, can lead to social isolation from colleagues.

In about 30 per cent of cases the problems associated with gambling have led to resignation or termination of employment. Resignation is a step taken by many to avoid being detected or prosecuted for misappropriation, embezzlement or theft from petty cash. One gambler employed as a car parts salesman reported persistently stealing and selling spare parts to acquaintances to finance his gambling. This occurred in all three jobs he held in that industry and again in another non-related industry before he was caught and charged. His pattern was to leave each job as soon as he believed his supervisors suspected that he was the culprit.

What is of especial interest is the amount of time and effort some people are prepared to put into gambling and losing money, while avoiding placing a similar amount of effort into their work, which should be personally and financially more rewarding. Some gamblers show exceptional talents that, if directed to their work, would result in personal satisfaction and significant business success. Stephen was an accountant of outstanding abilities who, over a period of two years, embezzled one hundred thousand pounds from his computer company. Only a small fraction of his fraud was detected, and that only by accident. It was only when he cooperated with the police and his auditors that the true extent and ingenuity of his crime were discovered. He then proceeded to instruct his employers on how to strengthen the security of their accounting system to prevent future fraud. The company was impressed with his knowledge and hard work and offered him a job on his release from prison – but of course with restricted access to cash, 'just to be safe and for peace of mind,' said the general manager.

Lying and Deceit

'Lying is a way of life now. It's easier to tell my husband I've been visiting Jill and a few of the mothers from pre-school than telling him that I spent several hours playing bingo.'

The further the gambler moves towards the desperation phase of gambling, the greater is the pressure to conceal their behavior, so that lying becomes an automatic part of everyday living. Lies become more frequent as the gambler attempts to explain: unaccounted time away from the family or work, lack of money to pay bills, mood swings, and phone calls from creditors.

Additional pressure is placed on the gambler after domestic arguments and promises never to gamble again. The following cycle is so commonly described that it almost appears to be a universal truth. First comes the promise to change. This is followed by a short period of improvement, then by more gambling. Once a gambling episode has occurred, there is pressure to keep losses hidden and to gamble more to win back the money before the loss is detected. The gambler cannot afford to disclose the lapse to his/her spouse because of the promise already made. Then comes discovery: the cover has been blown. Arguments ensue; the gambler expresses remorse and promises never to gamble again – with an assurance that this time it is really genuine. And so the cycle begins again.

What is important is that gamblers trapped in this repeated cycle have not yet learnt the necessary skills and strategies that will assist them in identifying the steps leading to a relapse and taking alternative positive action that will immediately reduce their motivation to resume gambling. I have found that the person who responds well to therapy is the one who tells his or her spouse openly of an urge to gamble as soon as it is felt. The very act of admitting the impulse to one's spouse is often sufficient to abort the urge. Another benefit of open and honest communication is that one's partner is kept informed of what is happening and therefore soon begins to regain trust. It is the uncertainty of knowing whether or not one's spouse is gambling and what debts are being accumulated that is so stressful and distressing.

Cognitive Impairment

'Cognitive functioning' is a term used to refer to one's intellectual activity, which includes thinking, memory, problem-solving, concentration and reasoning. It is only to be expected that stresses resulting from the conflict over the simultaneous urge to gamble and awareness of the need to stop, the persistent worries over the problems being caused by gambling, and the fear of being found out, will lead to problems in these areas. There is interference in one's ability to think clearly, make decisions with confidence and retain new information. Forgetfulness is common; in some cases, concentration and attention are so poor that the person has difficulty reading and understanding newspapers or following the plot of a television show. These symptoms are related to stress and with proper management can be quickly reversed.

Physical Symptoms

The pathological gambler's physical health deteriorates rapidly under conditions of chronic stress: juggling disappearing finances, hiding evidence of all gambling activity and debts, chasing losses and attempting to maintain some semblance of normality to others. Headaches, high blood pressure, anxiety symptoms, fatigue and poor sleep are symptoms commonly reported. People just feel down, washed out and physically exhausted, with general complaints of aches and pains.

What is the Effect on the Gambler?

We know that constant worry and anxiety can eventually lead to stress-related physical symptoms. Symptoms of this kind, resulting from an underlying psychological stress, constitute what is called psychosomatic illness. The most commonly reported symptoms are:

- headaches;
- high blood pressure;
- gastro-intestinal problems such as nervous diarrhoea;
- general muscular aches and pains;
- other specific problems such as skin rashes.

Tackling the underlying stress by, for example, using the relaxation and other techniques described in Part Two of this book, can rapidly alleviate these distressing physical conditions.

5

What is the Impact of Problem Gambling on Family Members and Others?

The impact of gambling on the welfare of the gambler's partner and family can be extensive. The consequent financial difficulties in particular cause strain and friction within the family. Often the partner experiences a sense of betrayal, anger or despair and may suffer stress-related disorders. In a study of the spouses of gamblers, Valerie Lorenz, an American therapist, found that many reported suffering multiple psychosomatic symptoms including headaches, gastrointestinal disturbances, poor sleep and general malaise, and frequently consulted their family doctor. Sexual relationships, too, deteriorated as a result of a lack of communication, pervasive tension, unexpressed feelings of anger and low self-esteem.

What is most disappointing for many spouses is that apart from the gambling behavior, they love their partners and see them as wonderful and caring persons. If only the gambling stopped, they say, their relationship would be ideal. Perhaps this explains why many spouses stay with and support their partners despite their repeated broken promises and continued gambling. But while the gambling goes on, domestic arguments frequently occur. Conflicts arise as a result of the stress caused by continual financial difficulties and by the accompanying frequent lies to conceal the level of gambling going on.

Children in such living circumstances suffer considerably when exposed to a climate of tension, arguments and hostility, leading them to display signs of disturbed conduct and behavior. The effects of gambling on children are poorly researched, but we have a good understanding of the child's reaction to family arguments and to parental separation: the child responds with confusion, depression and a sense of low self-worth. The gambler is often absent but when present, is irritable, edgy and withdrawn. Constant arguments between parents create an environment of tension and fear. Tragically, some studies have shown that possibly a fifth of problem gamblers perpetrate acts of child physical abuse or domestic violence against their wives.

In summary, marital friction is shown in:

- frequent arguments between couples;
- the gambler's withdrawal from family outings and inter-actions;
- lack of funds for family activities;
- abusive behavior by the gambler;
- periods of marital separation;
- divorce.

It is clear that excessive gambling will eventually result in the build-up of debts that cannot be met. The lack of available money to meet the basic costs of daily living expenses and fixed repayments results in the family not being able to:

- pay for emergency/unexpected repairs to house or car;
- meet rent/mortgage payments and utility bills;
- afford family holidays;
- afford social or leisure activities for family members;
- purchase gifts for special occasions;
- have enough disposable income for occasional extra needs.

The constant financial pressure increases the stress on the gambler, who becomes ever more worried and preoccupied as a result, and consequently ever more detached from the family and particularly sensitive to any questions that may be raised regarding the household's financial condition. Outbursts of irritability and anger become commonplace.

Eventually access to money is limited, forcing the gambler to seek other sources of funds. These include:

- spending savings (own or spouse's);
- cashing assets such as pension funds, shares or bonds;
- cashing in holiday and/or sick pay allowances;
- drawing cash advances from credit card accounts;
- taking out high-interest loans;
- pawning jewellery and electrical goods;
- accessing bank accounts of family members without their knowledge;
- engaging in criminal activities such as embezzlement, theft or burglary.

In the vast majority of cases, the spouse is unaware of what is happening and of the level of financial debt.

To avoid detection the gambler begins to be deceitful and dishonest, resorting to frequent lies and excuses explaining why bills are not paid or purchases/holiday cannot be afforded.

The following are some of the many stratagems used by gamblers to conceal problems from their families:

- inventing excuses as to why they cannot afford purchases;
- redirecting bills to post office boxes so that the spouse remains unaware of unpaid or overdue bills;
- intercepting the mail before the spouse has a chance to see what is coming in to the household;
- refusing to allow the spouse to open mail;
- picking up bank statements directly from the bank;
- forging the spouse's signature on loan applications or other documents;
- pawning items of value and then claiming these to be lost or stolen.

These stratagems may be successfully applied for several years, with partners, family members and relatives remaining oblivious to their deteriorating financial circumstances. At times a partner may be perplexed and worried over the gambler's

54

behavior; often, too, lack of interest in him- or herself or in the family, a preoccupied manner, lack of money, and time spent away from home may lead a partner to assume that the gambler is having extramarital affairs or has a problem with alcoholism.

Discovery of the true situation often comes alarmingly suddenly and from unexpected sources:

- bank statements revealing large loans or overdue bills;
- deposit account statements revealing the loss of savings and assets;
- credit card statements showing frequent and large cash advances;
- pawn tickets for items claimed to have been lost or stolen;
- forged signatures on documents;
- police visiting to interview the gambler or to level charges for offences committed;
- receipt of legal notices threatening repossession or similar action.

A Spouse's Reactions to the Discovery of Gambling Debts

Spouses go through a series of complex and confusing emotions as they become aware of what is happening behind their backs. Their dreams, expectations and future plans are shattered as they realize that they are no longer in a financially secure position. What is most damaging and challenging is confronting the reality that the person to whom they are married and on whom they thought they could depend has been repeatedly deceitful and playing them for a fool. Trust of any type has evaporated.

A spouse may experience a mixture of distressing emotions or may go through a process in which a series of feelings emerge over time. There is no consistent pattern, but the predominant sequence is as follows.

Confusion
- Stunned disbelief of what has happened.

- Questioning if it is really happening or whether some unfortunate mistake has occurred.
- Self-doubt: 'Is it my fault? Did I cause him/her to gamble?'

Guilt

- 'I should have picked up the signals earlier.'
- 'If only I had realized then I could have prevented this situation.'
- 'It was my behavior or our relationship that caused him/her to gamble, I did not give him/her enough attention.'

Anger

- 'How could he/she do this to our family?'
- 'I have worked hard to save or to enable him/her to save for a new house or holiday and now he/she has lost it all.'
- 'How could he/she be so selfish as to spend our hard-earned money on himself/herself in such a useless activity?'

Loss of Trust

- 'I can no longer trust him/her.'
- 'What else has he/she done behind my back?'
- 'How can I ever believe what he/she tells me?'

Worry for the Future

- 'What does this mean for the future?'
- 'How can we get ourselves out of this situation?'
- 'How will I get a job to help keep our heads above water?'
- 'Is he/she going to gamble again and cause further problems?'

The most worrying aspect is the loss of trust – the very foundation of any marital relationship. With lack of trust comes uncertainty: uncertainty as to whether you know the whole picture or whether there are other similar problems remaining that the gambler has yet to reveal. This uncertainty is reinforced when newer debts or problems are revealed. Most spouses don't know the full extent of the problems generated by their partners' excessive gambling, and they live in constant fear and suspense that another major crisis will reveal itself shortly.

The other major uncertainty is the question of continued gambling. Having deceived the spouse in the past, will the gambler again at some future point recommence gambling and plunge the household into another downward spiral of financial woes?

With the lack of trust and uncertainty come strong feelings of insecurity and fear.

The typical response of the gambler to discovery is to deny or minimize the situation by arguing that the situation is not as bad as it appears, that they have a plan of action which will get them out of their problems or that this is a 'one-off' aberration that they will never repeat. Many gamblers show remorse and contrition, promising fervently that they will never repeat their mistake or gamble again.

If the spouse reacts with anger, the gambler may defend him- or herself by manipulating emotions. She/he may attempt to transfer guilt and blame to the spouse by arguing that it was his/her fault that she/he gambled in the first place. He/she may act as the victim and attempt to draw sympathy and concern from the wife or husband. Alternatively, he/she may act helpless and dependent, eliciting emotions of sympathy and sorrow for his/her plight. By so doing, the cause of the problem is again shifted from the gambler to his/her partner, who is now seen as being responsible for the excessive gambling and therefore responsible for solving the problem.

This self-help book may assist a gambler's spouse, close friend or employer to understand the nature of gambling. Partners may also need assistance and guidance in learning how to deal with the stresses of their situation and advice on how to respond to demands placed on them. It is advisable for them to seek help from Gam-Anon, a self-help organization aimed at helping the partners of pathological gamblers, or treatment from qualified clinical psychologists, psychiatrists or other health professionals such as general practitioners or social workers familiar with the problems of pathological gambling. Referral to these specialists may be sought from local community health service facilities. Gam-Anon meetings are held at the same time as the Gamblers Anonymous meetings for the gambler. Details of meetings can be obtained from the Gamblers Anonymous contact number listed in your local telephone directory.

Gamblers, Crime and the Law

In one of the saddest cases I have come across, Morris, a fifty-nine-year-old librarian, was addicted to slot-machine gambling for ten years. He resorted to any means possible to obtain money. Once he paid a woman he met on the street to pretend to be his wife while he extended a loan from an account jointly held with his wife. What really undermined his self-esteem and caused his depression to plummet was another episode in a club where, as he walked past a woman sitting at a table, he quickly kicked her handbag away, picked it up and took it to the toilet where, quivering with anticipation, he rummaged through the purse and removed all the money. The bag also contained a passport and other important documents, but at the time the anxiety and inconvenience he was creating for the bag's owner was of little concern to him: he thought no further than satisfying his own needs. Only later, in the calm of the aftermath did the full impact of his action bring him down emotionally. Even so, several days later he shamefully confessed that he was out looking for a similar opportunity when he needed money again. Guilt dissolved in the face of gratifying his needs.

Morris is not an isolated instance. Research has revealed that 60 per cent of pathological gamblers commit some criminal offence in order to support their gambling habits. The gravity of these offences range from theft from their partner's bank account or writing cheques knowing that there are insufficient funds in the account, through taking money from petty cash through to serious and premeditated fraud and embezzlement. It is sobering to note that 22 per cent of pathological gamblers have been charged for offences, and 12–15 per cent have been convicted of such offences.

Gamblers commit criminal offences when legal sources of funds are totally exhausted and to enable them to:

- continue the gambling habit;
- attempt to recoup losses;
- repay money borrowed from friends;
- meet repayments to financial institutions for loans taken out;
- obtain money to repay debts and cover shortfalls incurred because of gambling;
- cover up losses and avoid detection by partner, employer or friends.

Typically, it is found that the gambler commits about ten offences involving amounts of one hundred and fifty pounds each. However, it is worth noting that 15–20 per cent engage in offences relating to amounts of ten thousand pounds or more. I have known of or personally treated at least ten gamblers who have appeared in court for offences involving sums exceeding one million pounds.

What is tragic is that the majority of gamblers who offend show no evidence of any other criminal behavior and do not have a past history of anti-social behavior or conflict with the law. It is clear from research data that most gamblers are led into crime as a result of their excessive gambling and the need to cover it up. This, of course, enables them to argue that they are not fully responsible for their own behavior; and yet gamblers *do* know what they are doing and *are* aware that what they are doing is wrong. Consequently, they cannot argue that they should have consideration at law on account of a condition called 'pathological gambling'.

Some gamblers fall foul of the law when they forget, or are unaware, that some behavior may be regarded by some people as acceptable when it is technically illegal. We have had two or three cases where a person was in serious trouble for failing to bank income from sales on the Friday, using the money to gamble over the weekend and then replacing the funds later the following week. Their employers laid charges against them for unauthorized use of company money. The rule is simple: if it is not yours, then do not spend it; and gambling is spending.

Social Problems

Gambling has a major impact on social and family life, affecting not only the gambler but, most importantly, the spouse or partner and children, not to mention other relatives including parents. The preoccupation with gambling, fear that others may discover the true extent of one's behavior and financial predicament all motivate the gambler to shun social contact. Social occasions that conflict with gambling opportunities are avoided. Excuses are made not to attend or, if attending, to leave at odd times so that bets may be placed. Family outings, especially on Saturdays, no longer happen. No efforts are made to go out to restaurants, shows or indeed any activities that cost money that otherwise could be gambled. The preoccupation with gambling virtually eliminates any enjoyment of or motivation to participate in non-gambling-related leisure pursuits. Repeated refusals of invitations to go out with friends lead to such invitations becoming fewer and less frequent. Marital arguments over financial matters and gambling make it unpleasant for the couple to be together in public, and to avoid embarrassment it is much easier to remain at home. Others feel uncomfortable to be around a couple who are always arguing.

Because of the social embarrassment of not having enough money to buy clothes and goods, the partner of a gambler may not wish to talk to friends, and may instead avoid any situation where such subjects are raised and where it might be necessary to lie in order to cover up the true situation.

These circumstances lead to:

- social withdrawal and isolation;
- loss of friends;
- reduced motivation for activities other than gambling;
- irritability, tension and moodiness when pressured to attend social functions that interfere with gambling.

The overall picture of the gambler and his or her family is an unhappy one. But, as we shall see in the next chapter and in Part Two of this book, it is possible successfully to treat problem gambling, to the great and lasting benefit not only of gamblers but of those around them too.

6

How Can Problem Gambling be Treated?

Effective treatment of problem gambling is still in its infancy. But it must be stressed that it *is* treatable and that many people are able to improve their quality of life as a result of undertaking treatment. No matter how desperate the situation may seem at the time, by taking the proper steps outlined in Part Two of this book, control over behaviour can be regained.

Psychological Treatments

Several psychological treatments have been used to help people with gambling problems. Between 1914 and 1957 the only approach offered by mental health professionals was psycho-analytic or psychodynamic in orientation. It was argued that gamblers had an unconscious drive to punish themselves as a result of unresolved Oedipal complexes. The few case studies reported in the literature were not systematically evaluated over reasonable follow-up periods.

Two important events in the late 1950s and early 1960s, one in the USA and the other in the UK, had an important influence in shaping the direction of gambling treatment. First, Gamblers Anonymous was established in 1957. This is a self-help group based on the same philosophy and approach as Alcoholics Anonymous. This organization worked closely with the late Dr Robert Custer, a psychiatrist who established the first hospital gambling program at the Veterans' Administration in Brecksville, Ohio in 1972. Through Dr Custer's efforts, compulsive or pathological gambling came to be recognized as a psychiatric disorder in 1980.

Because of the close association between GA and Custer's program, compulsive gambling in America quickly came to be regarded as an addiction. Most programs to treat it are now offered in drug and alcohol facilities and place a heavy emphasis on attendance at GA meetings.

The second event was a sad case of brain surgery carried out in the UK. A twenty-one-year-old Cheshire ice-cream seller was convicted of stealing to support a gambling habit. The magistrate, with the agreement of the patient and his mother, referred the matter to a neurosurgeon, who performed psychosurgery on the man. No records remain of the case but this radical form of intervention caused an uproar within the mental health field. This controversy prompted several British psychologists and psychiatrists to turn to behavioral treatments, in particular aversion therapy. In this form of therapy, mild electric shocks are given to the fingers while a person plays the slot machines or watches a horse race. Shocks may be administered randomly during various stages of slot-machine play, reading racing form guides, watching audio-visually presented gambling stimuli, or reading gambling-related phrases written on cards. The shocks delivered to the fingers are of an unpleasant but not painful nature. The idea is to form a new association between an activity that was previously pleasurable and an aversive or unpleasant stimulus. While effective with about up to a quarter of gamblers, the technique involved the infliction of pain and was not very popular with many therapists.

More recently, cognitive behavioral therapy coupled with relapse prevention techniques are proving to be a highly effective alternative treatment route. Part Two of this book concentrates on cognitive behavioral techniques in the management of problem gambling. The rest of this chapter outlines the cognitive behavioral approach to therapy and describes briefly the role that can be played by medication, particularly in light of recent psychopharmacological advances in drug therapy. Additional detailed information on the foundation of cognitive-behavior therapy as applied to pathological gambling can be found in Michael Walker's comprehensive book, *The Psychology of Gambling* (see the section on Useful Reading at the end of this book).

How Do Gamblers Think?

'Cognitions' are mental activities such as thoughts, beliefs, attitudes, images and memories, which together form a person's schema or mental representation of the self, others and the world in general. A schema contains an organized set of core beliefs about specific things. For example, a gambler may view him- or herself as someone who has fewer skills and abilities than others but has high expectations to succeed placed on them by parents. Statements may include: 'I must please my parents otherwise they will reject me as a worthless person'; 'To be accepted I must provide my children with whatever they want, a new computer, holidays, etc.'; 'Gambling is one way of getting money quickly so I can impress my wife by giving her what she wants.'

It is by identifying and correcting distorted or irrational ways of thinking that a person can start to take proper steps to overcome gambling. For example, a typical statement given by many gamblers in debt is: 'I owe so much I will never pay it off by working. The only way I can get enough money is by winning at the races.' They forget that gambling created the debt in the first place. If gambling led you to debt, then how will more gambling eliminate your debt? Surely, the end result of more gambling can only be an increase in how much you owe.

Here is another good example of how differently from non-gamblers gamblers think. The odds of winning a lottery may be two million to one. A non-gambler would say to him- or herself, 'The odds are against me, I am unlikely to win so I won't buy a ticket.' A gambler would say, 'Hey, someone has to win, that someone could be me. You've got to be in it to win it. I've been close several times, it must be my turn to win soon.' Advertisements promoting gambling emphasize this point by suggesting that everyone can be a winner, and exhorting you not to miss your turn.

What is Cognitive Therapy?

Although there are a number of different cognitive models, the common thread shared by all is that cognitions directly influence your behavior, that automatic thoughts can be brought to conscious awareness and monitored, that irrational cognitions can be altered and that altering such cognition leads to changes in one's behavior. What is an automatic thought? It is fascinating to note that many people are not consciously aware of the thought processes that operate to influence behavior. An automatic thought is literally a habit, a thought that occurs so often and so fast that you no longer become aware of its existence. Let me illustrate with an example. How many times have you driven a car and, while driving, become so engrossed in your own thoughts that you drive several miles without really concentrating on what you were doing? This is a normal phenomenon. You were able to change gears, watch out for traffic, and safely control the car. Yet you were not consciously aware of your actions while driving. You were relying on automatic reactions that allowed you to do one thing while being mentally preoccupied with something else.

The same applies in gambling. Decisions are made which lead one to 'suddenly' find oneself in a gambling setting. One does not remember how one came to be there. This is an example of automatic thinking.

In principle, therefore, the aim of cognitive therapy is to assist the gamblers in setting about systematically identifying distorted or irrational thoughts, challenging these faulty assumptions and replacing them with correct styles of thinking.

Distorted Thinking in Problem Gamblers

Let us briefly look at some of the more common faulty thoughts and ways of thinking that lead people to continue gambling despite the obvious problems it creates. The steps showing how one may correct these will be provided in more detail in Part Two of this book.

Most gamblers like to believe that they have some skill or

ability to influence the outcome of a chance event. The roulette player will study the pattern of numbers and place bets accordingly, the slot-machine player believes that pressing the button with a certain pressure will influence the spin, and lottery players will have their favourite winning numbers. There is some research evidence to support the notion of what E. J. Langer has called the 'illusion of control' – the belief that a gambler can alter the outcome of a chance event. It is related quite closely to superstitious behavior, that is, carrying a lucky charm which the gambler believes gives him or her an additional edge to influence the outcome.

Illusions of control are strengthened by a process of what the American psychologist Thomas Gilovich calls 'biased evaluation'. Simply put, this means that people will remember and recall wins more than losses, and will further attribute wins to their own skill or ability. Losses are easily forgotten, pushed out of mind or explained away as the fault of some other unforeseen influence. How many times have you heard the statement, 'The horse would have won had it not stumbled at the starting gate,' or 'The jockey was obviously holding him back'? However, when a long shot comes in, one always accepts that it is because of skill and good judgment, not pure luck or a fluke: 'I knew it would win, that's why I bet on it at such long odds.' The win serves to strengthen belief in one's own level of skill.

Many gamblers profess a solid knowledge of the mathematics of chance, but their behavior does not reflect it. Playing roulette, a gambler will not bet on a number that has just come up because they believe it has a lower probability of coming up twice in a row. Similarly, in tossing a coin, if five heads in a row are tossed, most people will argue that the next toss will have a higher probability of coming up tails. This is incorrect. The next toss will have a one in two chance of a head or tail irrespective of how many heads came before it. The toss of a coin is not dependent on what came up the toss before; any two tosses are mutually independent events.

In picking lottery numbers, say a series of six out of forty, most people will pick evenly spread numbers, for example, 1, 9, 15, 21, 34, 39. They believe that a series such as 1, 2, 3, 4, 5, 6 has a very much lower chance of coming up than one which is more evenly spread. This is wrong. Both series have as much chance as each other of coming up. Indeed, numbers picked at random do not show a consistent pattern of being evenly spread out but tend to cluster together; for example, all six numbers may be under 20, or there may be a sequence of two or three consecutive numbers such as 12, 13, 14. Try it and see.

Some gamblers will personify a favourite machine. By this I mean that they will start to talk to it as though it were a real being with whom they are interacting: 'Come on baby, this time you've got to give it to me'; 'What's wrong, have I upset you?'; or 'Damn you, let me win or I won't ever play you again.'

Some gamblers believe that they can win at gambling. These gamblers will usually relate a story of how they won a large amount of money. This proves that they can win, they say. But when you ask them what they did with the winnings, most say they re-gambled it, or bought something which they then had to pawn to get more money to gamble. What they need to do is to increase the time frame they are considering. For example, if a person enters a session with one hundred pounds, wins a million pounds, continues gambling and at the end of the session leaves with fifty pounds in his pocket, how much has he won (or lost)? The hard-core gambler would say he won a million pounds, the realist would say he lost fifty pounds.

It is important to realize that distorted cognition may play a part at any stage of the gambling cycle. It may lead you to believe that you have a much greater level of skill or control in influencing outcomes than you really have. It may lead you to filter out losses you had and to recall instead only the wins, giving you a wrong impression of having won more than you lost. It may influence the strength of your belief that you are about to win because of the number of close calls you've had. Machine manufacturers use this tendency to manipulate your behavior. Every so often a near-winning combination appears, giving rise to the expectation that the jackpot is due very soon. Nothing is further from the truth.

This is a carrot to keep you involved and playing. Such 'near wins' also lead the gambler to think that a losing streak is about to end.

Additional cognitive distortions can be found where the gambler has an over-optimistic belief in her own luck, for example, that things always turn out in her favour eventually. These people may be superstitious. How many times have you repeated a pattern of doing something, worn some favourite piece of clothing or item, sat at the same seat at bingo or always played your 'own' favourite machine? Some people will carry lucky charms or a lucky coin, or go through a ritual of touching a part of the machine to guarantee themselves good luck. While realizing that such behavior is superstitious and does not really influence outcome, people still hold these beliefs and practise these habits 'just in case; after all it doesn't do any harm.'

A few people, perhaps more than we imagine, hold a strong belief that they somehow have a greater level of inbuilt special skills, knowledge or other natural talents that give them a winning 'edge' over other gamblers. This applies more to people who gamble frequently. Their level of skill varies but it has been shown that many, in particular the younger gamblers, make reference to knowledge or familiarity with reel positions on fruit machines and the manual operations of buttons. They believe that they have better skills and a better chance of winning than others. It is interesting to see that belief in one's skill and ability to win persists despite the obvious evidence of continued losses. This is because people dismiss losses by attributing them to other factors: for example, someone else played the machine and broke the sequence.

Correcting one's core beliefs about gambling and about the chances of winning is crucial to overcoming uncontrolled gambling. However, there are a number of other factors that need to be taken into account and modified. One needs to be taught how to control the urge to gamble once it arises. Use of relaxation-based techniques, as described in Part Two of this book, is fundamental to success. Where depression occurs, one must take steps to reduce the low mood in order to increase motivation, the chances of compliance with treatment instructions and the hope that gambling and gambling problems can be overcome and solved. Use of medication under your family doctor's or psychiatrist's direction may be beneficial. Strategies to avoid exposure to gambling triggers may need to be applied. For those who suffer from an additional problem of alcohol or drug dependence, it is imperative that some help is directed to overcoming this problem, because it will determine how successful your efforts will be to regain control over gambling. All of these factors need to be addressed. By following each and every step in this self-help book, as well as possibly consulting other relevant books in this series and seeking help from your family doctor or community health centre, you will have set yourself on the pathway to recovery.

Medications

A limited range of medications are used in the treatment of pathological gambling. These drugs are helpful because of their indirect effect on improving mood or reducing impulsivity, but very little useful information about their effectiveness is available. Remember, there is no drug that eliminates the urge to gamble altogether. Medication therapy should not be used alone but in conjunction with other, psychological approaches, such as the cognitive behavioral approach described in this book.

Some studies have found lithium carbonate to be mildly beneficial in moderating mood fluctuations which appear linked to gambling behavior. Some people suffering mania or hypomanic episodes experience elevated mood, exaggerated feelings of confidence and impaired judgment which may result in prolonged episodes of excessive gambling. To illustrate, one police constable would periodically engage in severe bouts of gambling when he was in a high mood. He spent a whole week gambling virtually non-stop, amassing debts of several thousand pounds but confident in the belief that he would become a millionaire. He took out substantial loans and pawned jewellery. These cases are usually easy to identify because of the bizarre or unusual pattern of behavior.

The main use of medication, however, is to control depression. Anti-depressant drugs, such as the tricyclics (e.g. imipramine, amitriptyline) or monoamine oxidase inhibitors (e.g. phenelzine), are useful where the depression is so severe that it represents a risk of suicide. In other circumstances the gambler may be so depressed that any motivation to comply with therapeutic instructions is lost, or the future is seen as so bleak that any effort to resolve problems seem futile. If you suffer from depression, it is important to consult your family doctor for advice on whether an antidepressant medication may be of benefit.

The new generation of selective serotonin re-uptake inhibitors (SSRIs) merits special mention. A number of biological studies have indicated possible evidence for disturbances in the regulation of certain classes of brain neurotransmitters (serotonin, dopamine and noradrenaline). These naturally occurring brain substances regulate arousal, mood, impulsivity and responses to reward and punishment. Studies from my clinic have shown that gamblers obtain high scores on psychological measures of impulsivity, that is, making quick decisions without worrying about their consequences. There appears to be a positive association between impulsivity and level of gambling: that is, the higher the score on psychological measures of impulsivity, the greater is the severity of the disturbance caused by excessive gambling. Also, a high proportion of gamblers suffer significant depression; and it has also been proposed that some people use gambling as a means of overcoming their depression. Although there are a few reports in the literature suggesting that the SSRI medications are effective, it remains unclear whether they work by reducing the depression or by their action in dampening impulsivity.

Dr Eric Hollander has noted the similarities between impulse control disorders, including gambling, and other repetitive behaviors, including eating disorders and obsessive-compulsive neurosis. He and his colleagues argue that pathological gambling lies along part of an obsessive-compulsive spectrum of disorders. As a result of this hypothesis, medications used to treat obsessional disorders (e.g. clomipramine and SSRIs) have been used to treat gamblers.

Do consult your psychiatrist or family doctor who will guide you as to the most suitable medication for your individual needs.

7

The Goals of Treatment: Abstinence or Control?

A large percentage of gamblers are in conflict when it comes to goals of treatment, torn between a strong desire to continue and an equally strong aversion to the concept of completely giving up gambling. Why is this?

The Gambler's Dilemma

There are several reasons for this ambivalence. As we have already noted, gambling is an intrinsically exciting and physically arousing behavior. Laboratory studies have shown rapid increases in heart rate of up to 50 beats per minute under gambling conditions. One anecdote is worth describing here. I was conducting a study which was designed to investigate the role of endorphins, naturally occurring brain substances mimicking the effects of morphine, in producing 'highs' associated with gambling. Two subjects, having placed a bet, returned to the laboratory where an intravenous catheter was inserted into their arms to draw blood samples and their heart rate recorded while they listened to the race broadcast. During the broadcast, one subject's responses showed a marked increase as expected, but I was puzzled to find no increase in arousal in the other. When I questioned him, he informed me that the horse he had selected was a last-minute withdrawal and that he in fact had no bet resting on the outcome. While he listened with interest to the broadcast, he was not excited to anywhere near the same extent as his companion; the bet made all the difference.

Others are unable to consider ceasing gambling because they

become totally immersed in the activity to the exclusion of all other thoughts. All the sources of stress in their lives fade into the background as their focus of attention is narrowed on the task at hand: the act of gambling and the thrill of pursuing the next bet. Under such circumstances, gambling becomes a useful platform on to which one can escape from current emotional hassles and the anxieties of daily life. Gambling can also serve to alleviate boredom and depressed mood states. Many gamblers describe a feeling of elation when engaged in the process of gambling and in anticipation of the outcome. They participate because gambling makes them feel positive and happy, particularly during the intervening period between betting and awaiting the results; here they feel a lift in mood as they anticipate and daydream about a positive outcome.

The motivation to cease gambling is externally driven. It is true that a few gamblers are fully aware of their loss of control and realize that they must take action to prevent the development of significant problems in their lives. These people acknowledge that they are spending more time or money than they intended on gambling and that they have a sense of impaired control. They suffer a continual preoccupation with gambling and/or an inability to cease once they have commenced. Three-quarters of gamblers, however, are pressured to modify their behavior by their spouses, relatives or employers. These people are usually motivated by a desire to stop the gamblers developing significant problems in their lives, for example, marital tension, social isolation and loss of employment productivity, as a result of persistent losses.

Two Principles of Treatment

There are two main yet opposing principles of treatment proposed for problem gambling. In the first, the goal is 'abstinence'; in the second, it is 'controlled' gambling. Each will be discussed below. Gamblers Anonymous, as well as mental health and drug and alcohol treatment programs, advocate complete abstinence as the essential goal of any therapeutic intervention. Applied to gambling, abstinence is taken to mean absolutely no participation in any form of gambling on any level; this includes the occasional and infrequent purchase of raffle, lottery or scratch tickets, as well as entry into draws or office sweepstakes. According to this principle, then, the effectiveness of a treatment is based on very strict criteria. Abstinence is considered essential because of the strongly held belief that any episode of gambling, no matter how slight, will inevitably result in a relapse and resumption of compulsive gambling patterns. This belief is the same as that held for alcoholism and is reflected in the dictum of Gamblers Anonymous that compulsive gambling is a chronic progressive disorder that can never be cured but only arrested.

However, using abstinence as the only criterion for success in treatment ignores such important indices of improvement as reduced frequency of gambling, intensity and urge to gamble; enhanced ability to control gambling once commenced; and improved social, interpersonal and financial functioning.

A detailed reading of the psychological and psychiatric literature reveals that many outcome studies refer to marked reduction in the frequency and intensity of gambling after treatment. Positive gains are made despite the presence of continued gambling at much reduced levels. This has led several researchers to evaluate the effectiveness of controlled gambling. 'Control' in this context is used to describe a situation in which the gambler can place defined bets according to pre-arranged or agreed limits. In one case, a forty-four-year-old man with a twenty-year history of excessive gambling maintained control for almost all of the two-year follow-up period. In all the cases reported, the gambler's spouse was involved in financial management and supervision.

In a follow-up study over periods of from two to nine years, it was found that a third of gamblers achieved controlled gambling over a period of on average five years following behavioral therapy. This group showed a reduction on measures of psychopathology, gambling expenditure and debt, and at the same time improvement in overall quality of life, marital relationships and self-esteem. Importantly, a number of abstinent gamblers reported one or two lapses which did not lead to relapse or to a resumption of continued gambling. These episodes were confined to brief periods, less intense in magnitude and easier to overcome.

Should a gambler try for controlled gambling rather than abstinence to start off with in treatment? It can be argued that there are certain advantages in offering controlled gambling, particularly with those people who are poorly motivated or do not believe that they want to or are able to achieve the difficult task of giving up entirely. Offering controlled gambling may increase the chance that ambivalent gamblers:

- agree to seek treatment;
- enter treatment at an earlier stage in their career;
- accept treatment because they feel that that can reduce but not totally stop gambling;
- see control as a more realistic and achievable goal for themselves;
- don't drop out of treatment because of one or two lapses. With abstinence one lapse represents a failure, whereas with controlled gambling, one lapse means that you have to apply control strategies more effectively.

A word of caution is in order here. While there is some suggestion that controlled gambling may be possible, at this stage we do not know how to differentiate between those gamblers who can achieve control over their compulsive gambling habits and those who cannot. Nor do we know the factors that predict who will or will not resume compulsive gambling after a lapse. Therefore, it is imperative that gamblers accept the necessity of abstinence as the preferred objective in the first instance. Only once they demonstrate a capacity to eliminate their compulsive urges can they even begin to contemplate the notion of control. Even then, the advice must always be to avoid gambling. Why take the chance of exposing yourself to risk if you have already demonstrated a failure to retain control over behavior in the past?

Gamblers have a tendency to rationalize and justify much of their behavior. Cognitive distortions allow them to embark on a course of action that will eventually lead to their downfall – much in the same way as the alcoholic who convinces himself that he can visit his friends at the local pub without having a drink. He may be successful for a period, but then succumb to the temptation, usually feeling sure at that point that he can have one or two drinks without losing control. It is important for gamblers to have a strategy for dealing with the risk of relapses.

How Can Relapses After Treatment be Prevented?

Once you have regained control over gambling, the battle is not completed. The trick is making sure that you do not slowly fall back into the trap. You cannot be complacent. This does not mean that you will always suffer the disorder of compulsive gambling for the rest of your life. Research has shown that some people can maintain controlled gambling over a long period of time; but, as discussed previously, this is not an advisable goal to aim for in the first instance. People have a tendency to fall back into old practices over time and mistakenly believe that they have conquered or cured the problem. All too often, gamblers say, 'I have not had the urge to gamble now for the last six months or so. I'm in control. Let's test it out. I'll just enter the gambling arena and see how I feel. One bet is all I'll have. There's no harm in that, surely.' What is happening here is the first step in a series of apparently irrelevant decisions that will invariably lead to a fall.

Relapse prevention strategy has grown out of the study of addiction. Its main purpose is to teach people to see the chain of seemingly innocent links that gradually leads them to a high-risk situation where the likelihood of a relapse or 'bust' is greatly increased. One of the most important components of any treatment program is learning how to avoid the pitfalls that are likely to result in long-term failure. Once you have identified the conditions under which you are most likely to experience the urge to gamble or the triggers which cause a rise in your interest and urge, as well as the alternative steps to take to change your course of action, and have learned how to seek support from others close to you, you are well on the way to continued long-term recovery.

In essence, what you need to do is to learn a number of straightforward strategies that will:

- help you reduce your urge to gamble when it arises through a relaxation technique (imaginal desensitization);
- correct faulty logic and thinking processes that cause you to persist in the belief that you have special skills or control over the outcome of a chance event and that you can actually win at gambling over the longer term;
- learn to identify triggers that will provoke your urge to gamble in future, such as negative emotional states;
- learn stress management and problem-solving strategies that will give you alternative ways of dealing with stress, anxiety and depression;
- learn to avoid gambling-related cues that will fuel your desire to gamble.

Before moving on to the practical aspects of how to regain control over your gambling, we will next look briefly at some technical points related to problem gambling.

A Short Technical Note

It is well known that people have gambled since ancient Egyptian times, but it was only at the beginning of the twentieth century that psychologists and psychiatrists first showed any interest in the behavior. By the middle of the century, several treatments were being offered in self-help groups like Gamblers Anonymous or by psychologists and psychiatrists using behavioral and psychodynamic approaches, but it was not until 1980 that problem gambling came to be accepted as a major psychiatric disorder when it was included in the American Psychiatric Association's classification system, the *Diagnostic and Statistical Manual of Mental Disorders*, third edition (known as DSM-III).

Pathological Gambling: A Disease or a Social Problem?

No one is really clear about the nature of pathological gambling. The 'disease' model suggests that pathological gamblers are categorically distinct in some way from social gamblers and non-gamblers. This view is held by Gamblers Anonymous and health professionals who advocate classifying gambling as an addictive disorder. The opposing 'dimensional' approach argues that gambling lies on a continuum and that social and pathological gamblers represent extremes at each end of the spectrum. On this view, problem gambling is considered a social issue and not a psychological or psychiatric illness.

Although this debate continues, the American Psychiatric Association, in its most recent *Diagnostic and Statistical Manual of Mental Disorders* (DSM-IV, 1994), decided to regard gambling as a psychiatric condition but was not fully in favour of considering it a true addiction because there was no external substance involved. As a compromise, the decision was reached to include pathological gambling in the category of 'Disorders of Impulse Control Not Elsewhere Classified' alongside a range of seemingly unrelated problems such as intermittent explosive personality, compulsive shoplifting (kleptomania), fire-setting (pyromania) and hair-pulling (trichotillomania). Importantly, however, the diagnostic criteria for pathological gambling were deliberately and directly based on those used for the substance abuse disorders.

The Defining Features of a Disorder of Impulse Control

There are three main features which distinguish disorders of impulse control. These are (a) the repeated failure to resist an urge to carry out a behavior that is (b) preceded by an increasing sense of tension and (c) results in an experience of pleasure, gratification or release following its completion. These features are also found in the group of sexual deviation disorders that includes exhibitionism (flashing), voyeurism (peeping-tom) and paedophilia (child sexual abuse), a separate and distinct group of behaviors that is also characterized by recurrent impaired control over urges.

The Definition of Pathological Gambling

DSM-IV defines pathological gambling as persistent and re-current maladaptive gambling behavior which causes disruption or damage to several areas of a person's functioning, including personal, family or vocational pursuits. The gambling cannot be explained by a psychiatric condition of mania or a manic episode. In addition, at least five or more of the following features need to be present:

1 an excessive preoccupation with gambling;
2 a need to increase the amounts gambled to achieve desired excitement;

3 repeated unsuccessful efforts to cease gambling;
4 restlessness and irritability when gambling ceases;
5 gambling to escape problems or relieve negative moods, depression or anxiety; chasing losses;
6 lying to conceal debts from others;
7 committing illegal acts to support gambling behavior;
8 compromised or lost significant employment or vocational opportunities;
9 reliance on others to provide money to relieve financial crisis.

As mentioned above, the criteria have been deliberately based on those for the substance abuse disorders. Criterion suggests the concept of craving, criterion reflects the notion of tolerance and criterion 4 that of withdrawal symptoms. Some limited indications of withdrawal symptoms have been found in the handful of available studies which have shown that about a third of gamblers suffer headaches, gastrointestinal disturbances, irritability and sleeplessness in the period immediately after ceasing gambling. But more studies need to be carried out before it can be stated with any degree of confidence that withdrawal and tolerance are consistent features of problem gambling.

How Common is Pathological Gambling?

Only a small proportion of adults can be said to suffer problem gambling. Substantially more people engage in responsible gambling. Surveys in the UK, Australia and the USA reveal that between 30 per cent and 90 per cent of adults have gambled at one time or other in their lives, depending on the availability of gambling outlets in the community. The varying rate across countries is determined by the degree to which religious beliefs (on the part of, for example, Muslims or Jehovah's Witnesses) or laws (in, for example, Hawaii compared to Nevada) specifically restrict or ban gambling.

Estimates suggest that 40 per cent gamble regularly at least once a week. It can be stated that somewhere in the vicinity of 0.5–1.6 per cent of adults gamble excessively to the extent of meeting the formal diagnosis of pathological gambling. An additional 1–3 per cent are said to fall in the domain of 'probable' problem gambling, that is, they show some but not all signs of pathological gambling. Most pathological gamblers (about 75–85 per cent) are males, although data show a rising trend among females over the last ten years.

Where legal forms of gambling are available in the community, surveys reveal that 5–6 per cent of school-age adolescents meet the criteria for problem gambling. Indeed, 90 per cent of pathological gamblers begin in early adolescence, many starting to gamble as young as thirteen or fourteen years of age. While patterns vary considerably, with some gamblers becoming 'addicted' almost immediately after they first play, the general finding is that most are able to contain their gambling until the mid-twenties before losing control; many do not seek treatment until about ten or so years later, in their late thirties. The average age at which treatment is sought is thirty-five to thirty-nine years.

Pathological Gambling, Depression and Substance Abuse

Depression is commonly associated with problem gambling. About three-quarters of problem gamblers suffer severe depression, with about a fifth of these having serious suicidal thoughts or making a serious suicidal attempt. In a proportion, the depression is present before gambling commences. In these instances, gambling is used as a means of alleviating the depression, in much the same way that an alcoholic may drink to reduce anxiety.

For many, the stress and strain of constant financial worry, pressure to make ends meet, and fear of spouses, employers or the police finding out quickly takes its toll on mood and behavior. The gambler becomes withdrawn, distant, moody and irritable. In most instances, severe depressive episodes, and in particular suicide attempts, occur following the disclosure or discovery of major financial debts and/or criminal activity. The shock of such revelations devastates the spouse, who had until then remained totally unaware of any possible difficulties. The prospect of financial ruin, loss of assets including the home, legal action and loss of employment becomes emotionally overwhelming for all concerned. The loss of trust, intense anger and anxiety on the part of the spouse results in arguments and the threat of separation or divorce.

During this crisis period, anti-depressant medication is often useful to help improve mood and reduce the risk of impulsive suicidal gestures. Consult your family doctor or local community mental health service for advice on these matters.

It is not surprising, then, that rates of alcohol abuse and/or dependence in problem gamblers are high. Studies have repeatedly shown that approximately 20–30 per cent of problem gamblers show signs of excessive alcohol consumption. The precise pattern of association with actual gambling behavior is unclear; alcohol is consumed either before, during or after gambling. Where it occurs beforehand, alcohol may act to impair judgment and weaken inhibitions against gambling. A typical story is that of the gambler who enters a bar to drink socially with his friends. His resolve not to gamble gradually reduces in strength and he decides to try his luck with a few pounds. Very soon he finds himself having lost all his money gambling and becomes remorseful, guilty and angry, promising never again to place himself in that situation. This promise is repeatedly made and broken. After a gambling episode, alcohol is consumed to deaden pain and emotional distress.

The services of a drug and alcohol counsellor in your local health facility is often useful in helping to break out of this unrelenting cycle.

The self-help program outlined in Part Two of this book will help you regain control over your gambling habits. You may find it useful to supplement this by improving your own problem-solving and stress management skills and/or learning strategies to deal with depression by reading other self-help books in this series. Do consult your local family doctor or community mental health service for additional information on other treatment programs.

PART TWO

A Self-help Cognitive Behavioral Approach to Overcoming Problem Gambling

Introduction

There are a number of strategies that can be used to assist the motivated person in overcoming problem gambling. How difficult it is to accomplish this task depends upon how much effort is put into the attempt. Some people are ambivalent about really wanting to give up an activity that they really enjoy, or that serves a psychological purpose in helping them to avoid confronting emotional difficulties. Some gamblers may believe that compulsive gambling is an incurable condition, or may simply not be aware that effective treatments exist. Others may not genuinely want to stop but feel coerced into trying in order to please their partners or employers. And yet it is clear that problem gambling can be overcome, if one really wants to, by following the steps outlined in the chapters to come.

An Effective Self-help Approach

It is possible to overcome problem gambling by learning certain techniques and adopting more realistic attitudes and beliefs about the prospect of winning. For some, using the steps outlined in this self-help book is all that is needed; for others, the book may be best used in conjunction with more intensive treatment from a service offering specialist counselling in problem gambling or from local mental health professionals. Either way, it is often advisable to attend Gamblers Anonymous meetings to obtain additional guidelines and support. Its sister organization Gam-Anon is also a helpful source of support and information for spouses and partners of

A *Self-help Guide*

gamblers. Whichever path you take, this book can be the starting point for regaining control over your behavior.

An Important Note

If you are in a crisis situation and likely to panic in such a way that you may harm yourself, immediately consult a psychiatrist or your local family doctor, who will provide necessary care for you. Once the crisis has resolved itself and you are no longer in danger of self-harm, you can proceed to use this self-help book while continuing to receive professional help.

Who Will Benefit from this Self-help Book?

This book is intended primarily for people who are interested in regaining control over gambling urges and behavior which create problems in their life. It is also a useful resource for family members who wish to have additional information that may aid them in offering assistance to the gambler. Broadly speaking, there are several groups who should find this book to be of benefit:

- Those whose gambling has become excessive and as a result is causing distress to themselves or others close to them. The distress may be associated with financial difficulties, depression and anxiety, marital strain, threatened employment or legal action. The level of distress may vary from feeling constantly unhappy and under pressure to deeply depressed and suicidal. For many, professional help must be sought. For them, this self-help book can complement psychological treatment offered by professionals.
- Those who have ventured into problem gambling but are still at an early stage. These people have recognized the first warnings of danger – spending too much time or money gambling – but are not yet experiencing serious consequences. They may not need professional intervention at this stage and tend to respond extremely well to the instructions contained in this book. For them, this book

can act as a preventive measure saving them from economic and personal hardship.

- Those who move between controlled and problem gambling. A number of people are able to gamble socially for a period of time but then experience episodes where they go overboard and create problems. This book can teach them the skills necessary to recognize and limit the extent of their gambling when they begin to lose control.
- Those social gamblers who want to cut down their gambling to more acceptable levels. One does not have to have problems in order to benefit from this book! Some report no difficulty in controlling their behavior except under certain circumstances. They complain that they occasionally have minor difficulties stopping once they start. This book contains hints on how to identify high-risk situations and take preventive action.
- Family members and relatives who are seeking information and guidance on how best to encourage and support their loved one in the attempt to overcome problem gambling. The general principles outlined in this book should provide comfort and reassurance.

Who Should Seek Further Assistance?

As noted above, not all people who cannot control their gambling will find fully adequate help in this book; some may need additional professional assistance. As a general guide, the types of people who may require special attention are as follows.

- Those for whom gambling is not the primary problem. In some psychiatric conditions such as manic depressive disorder, schizophrenia or major depression, gambling is just one of several disordered behaviors present. In mania, for example, elevated euphoria and grandiose ideas lead to a sense of overconfidence in the possibility of winning, resulting in uncharacteristic or bizarre patterns of gambling behavior, while the sense of hopelessness associated with depression may cause one not to care about excessive losses. Where there is a suggestion of an underlying psychiatric condition, seek proper care from a psychiatrist or clinical psychologist. Medication is often a necessary part of treatment. Once the primary condition is treated, the gambling behavior may itself decrease spontaneously.

- Where suicide is a real threat – particularly where there is a combination of alcohol dependence and depression, and where there is a looming financial, legal or marital catastrophe. Here it is essential that proper medical attention be given to reduce the risk of self-harm as soon as possible. Teaching cognitive behavioral strategies to control gambling is temporarily set aside until the suicidal condition has stabilized. This self-help book can be introduced once the risk of self-harm is contained and under proper professional supervision.

- Those who suffer from alcohol dependency. About a fifth to a third of alcoholics have a coexisting gambling problem, while a similar proportion of gamblers suffer from alcohol dependency. Alcohol can very easily impair one's judgment and self-control. If you suspect you may have a drinking problem, it is strongly recommended that you seek treatment from your local drug and alcohol services counsellor. Two to four standard drinks is the suggested daily limit for alcohol consumption. If you consume more than this, it is wise to obtain professional advice.

- Those who are heavily pressured by their partner, employer or solicitor to seek help to reduce their gambling. These gamblers are generally resentful and, although agreeing to read the self-help book, fail to follow advice or apply the strategies outlined. In these circumstances motivation is low, compliance poor and, not surprisingly, success rare. For these people, the initial step must be individual sessions with a mental health professional aimed at motivating the gambler to stop. You cannot force change on an unwilling person, no matter how much you try. The best strategy is one of encouragement and support.

- A related group is those gamblers who flatly and consistently deny that they have a problem. Constantly confronting them leads only to arguments and continued denial. These people are just not interested in receiving help. Again, encouragement and support, not pressure and threats, are the responses most likely to maximize the possibility of a change in attitude.

- Where gambling is an expression of resentment, hostility and anger toward a partner. In some cases, a person may gamble excessively to get back at his or her partner for something they have done. A wife who finds out her husband is having an affair may subconsciously accelerate her gambling to get even with him by spending their savings, for example. Here, it is important to identify the underlying reasons for gambling and obtain appropriate marital or relationship counselling. The self-help book may assist in the process once the relationship conflicts are resolved.

- Those suffering brain injury or intellectual impairment. Brain damage or impairment may affect judgment, the degree to which behavior can be inhibited and the consequences of actions taken understood. In this context, the self-help book may provide excellent resource material to which the person can repeatedly refer; but it is necessary to make sure that the instructions are fully comprehended. Therefore, in these cases it may be useful to have a mental health professional familiar with brain or intellectual impairment guide the person through the steps outlined in the book.

Resistance to Change

The steps set out in the following chapters are designed to help you overcome your gambling problem. What is meant by overcoming your problem depends on what goal you wish to pursue – to become completely abstinent and never gamble again, or to reduce your activity to acceptable levels. To commit yourself to giving up entirely can be a difficult decision to take.

To help you make your decision, list here some reasons in

favour of and against giving up completely; now do the same for only reducing your level.

Reasons for:

Giving up gambling altogether	Simply reducing your level
_____	_____
_____	_____
_____	_____
_____	_____

Reasons against:

Giving up gambling altogether	Simply reducing your level
_____	_____
_____	_____
_____	_____
_____	_____

Whichever you choose, ultimately it means that you must give up or decrease an activity that may be highly exciting for you. This is a difficult choice, and one that some people try to resist for as long as possible. Excuses include that the problem is not really as bad as it seems, one will stop next week, or there is nothing comparable to replace the gambling. It is important to accept that gambling is creating hazards in your life, producing stress and affecting the happiness of your family. The longer you delay, the deeper will be the hole you have dug for yourself out of which you have to climb. Keep in mind that the quality of your life will be vastly improved if you accept the challenge of overcoming your gambling.

Preparing for Change

Sometimes there are a number of additional problems that need to be dealt with before the process of change outlined in this self-help book can be commenced. These are obstacles in the way of taking that difficult first step toward self-help.

Current Financial Problems

Most gamblers are in debt. Often the true level of debt is kept concealed from others. Part of the anxiety and pressure to gamble derive from the wish to win enough to repay debts before anyone finds out. The difference between a positive and a negative response to treatment often rests on how prepared one is to be open and honest with one's partner in revealing the full extent of existing debts. You will need to trust your partner that even though they may react with anger, they will respect you for coming clean. It is the lies, deceit and uncertainty that cause so much distress and suffering to partners.

The best thing to do, then, is to face the problem head-on and in full:

- Make a tally of all debts, whether owed to friends, banks, loan companies or credit card companies.
- Give your partner the details of all your debts.
- Do not try to conceal any debt. This only creates distrust later on when found out.
- Tell your partner that you wish to take full responsibility for repaying all debts.
- Arrange to have your pay deposited directly into your bank account.
- Ask your partner to help you work out a budget plan. Calculate your regular weekly income and expenditure. Put aside enough out of your income to pay all regular bills. Where possible, arrange direct automatic payments out of your account.
- Plan to pay off debts over time rather than immediately. Keep in mind that rushing to pay off debts only serves to make you think of returning to gambling as a quick fix solution. It won't work.
- Involve your partner as a support in helping you deal with your problem.

Terry was nine thousand pounds in debt. He panicked because he believed it would take him years to repay it. The thought of working hard just to give his earnings to someone else (in repaying debts) frustrated him. He felt he was getting nowhere. One large win would do the trick, he hoped. But the debt increased with each passing week. When he introduced a sensible budget designed to cover living costs and pay off part of his debt regularly, he was surprised to discover that it took only eighteen months to eliminate his debt completely. Seeing his debts slowly decreasing encouraged him enormously.

Sometimes it may be necessary to consult an accountant or financial advisory support service to obtain advice on how to plan a budget. These services will review your income and expenditure and work out the most efficient approach to managing your finances. Often, it is easier and cheaper to take out one loan to repay all outstanding debts rather than have multiple debts at high interest rates. An additional advantage of making use of these services is that they can negotiate with financial institutions to vary the terms of your loans to make them more manageable.

Receiving financial guidance is beneficial in giving one a sense of structure and control over a seemingly chaotic situation. Seeing a light at the end of the tunnel will increase your hope, confidence and motivation in overcoming gambling.

Legal Problems

A large number of gamblers commit offences as a means to supplement their gambling funds. This happens when they are no longer able to borrow money from legitimate sources. In the desperation phase, stealing petty cash, writing cheques with insufficient funds in the account and even forging signatures are common. In extreme cases, gamblers may engage in large-scale embezzlement or pushing drugs, as I have seen on several occasions. I have now treated more than half a dozen clients who have taken in excess of A$1 million from their employers.

For most gamblers, the slide into crime is gradual and unintentional. One small crime leads to another until finally they are in such dire straits that they believe that more gambling is the only path to salvation. Do not fall into this trap.

One fortunate client I saw recognized the danger signs and acted promptly to avoid the looming anguish. Jack, a forty-six-year-old hardware delivery driver, regularly collected cash from customers. He was in the habit of banking sales proceeds at the close of the day. One Friday, he was running late and missed the bank. He decided to keep the money over the weekend and deposit it first thing Monday morning. During the Saturday, he was given a sure tip on a horse. Not having his own cash available, he decided to take a hundred pounds out of money that needed to be banked. He did not realize that this is an illegal act. The horse lost – not by much, but that didn't make any difference. His employer's money was gone. He contemplated taking the remainder to see if he could win back the losses. Sensibly he resisted, told his boss on Monday morning what had happened, and agreed to a plan to repay the money. His employer then introduced a new set of guidelines for delivery drivers to prevent a similar circumstance from recurring and to take any further temptation away from Jack. Had Jack not made that decision to confess, I am sure that his situation would have deteriorated to the extent of possible police action being taken against him.

One needs to be aware that problem gambling is not a defence for diminished responsibility at law. In committing a crime, one is aware that what one is doing is wrong, and that one has full control over one's behavior. The strong urge is to gamble, not to commit a crime. In the same way, a heroin addiction is no excuse for committing a crime.

If you are committing offences to support your habit:

- Stop any further offences immediately. Ask yourself: Where will it lead? How long will it be before I get caught?
- Unburden yourself by discussing your actions with your partner. Once over the shock, a partner may provide good advice, help you make sensible decisions and offer strong support in dealing with the problem.
- Consider restitution and informing your employer. You need to repay all monies taken.
- Seek legal advice. If you have committed a major offence, do not continue in the hope of winning enough to cover your tracks and conceal the crime.

• Take responsibility for your actions. Even though it is an extremely difficult decision to take, accept the consequences of what you have done with the guidance of a solicitor. The alternative is living constantly in fear of discovery. Many a client suffers chronic anxiety, becoming jumpy and agitated every time the phone rings or a car pulls up outside their home. They report that when finally apprehended, a sense of relief is experienced: 'It is as though a weight was lifted off my shoulders.'

Substance Abuse

Gambling and substance abuse is a deadly combination. It aggravates existing problems and contributes to a worsening of depression, anxiety and low self-esteem.

Many gamblers turn to alcohol and drugs (both prescription medications and illicit drugs) to cope with stress and deaden the pain of guilt. Apart from the physical ill-effects of substance abuse, one's ability to think clearly and consider the consequences of actions is grossly impaired. Alcohol also reduces one's motivation and interferes with recovery. The will to resist urges is weakened, making a relapse more likely.

If you consume alcohol:

• Do not drink before or while you gamble.
• Avoid drowning your sorrows in drink after losing. Talk to your partner instead.
• If you are dependent, or others complain of your drinking, consult your local family doctor or community drug and alcohol service.
• If you are in a crisis and depressed, seek help immediately; do not rely on alcohol to see you through the day. Alcohol may increase the risk of self-harm in a moment of despondency and impaired judgment.

Marital Problems

Financial strain is a notorious cause of marital friction. Gamblers spend considerable time away from home, and when there are constantly moody and irritable with members of their family. Constant criticism and pressure from a partner to 'do something about your problem' merely aggravate the tension within the family. In couples where arguments are frequent and either partner is repeatedly having their inadequacies or past broken promises thrown in their face, they feel put down, unsupported and unvalued. Gambling is seen as a refuge from this situation and a way of dealing with the negative emotions.

If you are experiencing marital strain, it is wise to consult a relationship or marital counsellor at your local community health service. It is essential that you and your partner work in cooperation.

Gamblers often excel in shifting blame for their behavior on to others. Some common thought processes include:

- I gamble because my partner doesn't understand me.
- I gamble because my partner does not pay me enough attention.
- My partner's constant criticism or nagging forces me to gamble.
- My partner is no longer sexually attracted to me so I turn to gambling to make me feel better.
- My partner always wants things that I can't afford, so I gamble to try to win the money to buy them.
- My partner is always pestering me to do things, so I gamble to get away for peace and quiet.

The essential point to remember is that it is the gambler's choice to gamble: no one else's. No partner should feel guilty for being the so-called cause of their partner's gambling behavior.

Why do I have a Problem Gambling and Not Others?

True, most people are able to gamble socially without going overboard and getting into trouble. Some gamble excessively on occasion, that is, until they hit a certain level when they pull back. Some regular gamblers have a run of bad luck but are still able to contain their problems. Various possible explanations have been put forward as to why some people lose control and gamble excessively and others do not, but at present no one really knows. Reasons suggested by clinicians and researchers can be broken down into three broad categories: learnt behavioral habits, an addictive condition or an emotional response. One or a combination of these factors may contribute to loss of control.

Learnt Behavior Habits

A person may develop a habit through exposure to gambling and the excitement generated by winning. With repeated exposure, the habit strengthens and becomes part of one's lifestyle. Following a bout of losses which one can ill afford, attempts are made to recover the amount lost. Thus begins the process of chasing losses and the inevitable downward cycle into debt. At this point, problems develop and one has difficulty stopping.

An Addictive Condition

This is a controversial although popular conception of gambling held by many clinicians and Gamblers Anonymous. It is an attractive view of gambling because of the many similarities with substance addiction. However, while there are similarities, there are also many differences. In any event, some of the effective strategies applied in the treatment of addictions can be usefully applied in overcoming problem gambling: for example, the principles of relapse prevention established in the treatment of addictions form a strong therapeutic foundation for overcoming problem gambling. The main point to accept is that one is not suffering a disease over which one has no control. One cannot dismiss responsibility for one's gambling behavior by claiming one has an addiction.

Emotional Response

Stress, anxiety, depression and other negative emotional states may cause a person to increase gambling behavior. For these people, gambling serves as an emotional outlet or escape, or a means of avoiding having to deal with conflicts. They literally bury their heads in gambling. Poor stress management and/or problem-solving skills are a significant contributing factor to low mood and lack of self-esteem.

Irrespective of what you consider has contributed to the problem behavior in your case, there are strategies and techniques you can learn and follow that will help you overcome your gambling problems. Through improvement in your sense of self-control and self-esteem after learning the skills outlined in the following chapters, your quality of life will be considerably enhanced.

About the Self-help Program

The self-help guidelines set out in this book are designed to provide you with the necessary skills to regain control over your problem gambling behavior. The foundation of the program is the relaxation-based imaginal desensitization technique which several years of clinical research have shown to be highly effective in reducing compulsive and problem gambling habits. However, this skill is not learnt in isolation. Strategies designed to enable you to challenge your attitudes and beliefs about gambling and to identify and deal with high-risk situations are also described in some detail.

Not everything in this book will be of equal benefit to everyone. It is important to pick out those components which best apply to each individual's circumstances and to use those to maximum benefit. It is necessary to read and reread steps over a period of time to refresh your memory and sharpen up your skills. Each time you read the book, you may find something else to boost you along the road to recovery. It is important to use this book as a resource guide, referring to it whenever an occasion arises when there may be a risk, no matter how trivial it may seem, of a lapse looming ahead.

As with any learnt skill, it takes time and practice for successful results to be achieved. Overcoming ingrained habits and learning new habits does not occur overnight, so do not expect instantaneous results. A measured pace over time achieves the best results.

How this Self-help Book Should be Used

Read the book through once completely to get a general sense of what is required. Then go back to the beginning with the idea of taking one step at a time. Do not rush or skim the material, as you may miss important suggestions. It will take about one week for you to become familiar with the relaxation-based imaginal desensitization technique. After that, learning to identify irrational beliefs and ways to challenge these can take anywhere from one or two weeks to a month or so. There is no strict timetable; each person can and should work at his or her own pace. What is important is to work through the steps systematically and to revise steps at regular intervals. Do not become despondent if you do not respond immediately; it takes time and effort to get results. Progress is not necessarily smooth, so expect some setbacks as you go along. Learn from these by referring to the book and reviewing ways of handling these situations more effectively should they arise again in the future.

As you work slowly through each section, it is advisable to use paper and pencil to jot down your thoughts and ideas. Having something in writing allows you to compare notes to see how you are faring over time. Also, and importantly, it gives you the opportunity of showing others your thoughts about gambling. Feedback from others is a very useful way of challenging irrational thoughts and gaining suggestions on how to correct them.

Step 3 below involves the suggestion of tape-recording a series of habitual gambling practices and relaxation instructions which are read out aloud. Take time to do the recording and recruit the assistance of a partner to help supervise your practice session. Knowing that someone is monitoring practice sessions is a good way of maintaining motivation and momentum. Do not be afraid to discuss your concerns with the person offering supervision. He or she can provide alternative suggestions or pick up on irrational thinking styles. In addition, he or she can acknowledge successes and significant achievements that may be overlooked by yourself. Do not underestimate the importance of external praise in reinforcing your motivation and keeping up the impetus towards recovery.

As time goes on, you can become increasingly independent in recognizing danger signals and applying the skills you have learnt to continue on the road to recovery. The ultimate aim of this book is to teach you lifelong skills in controlling your behavior.

An Overview of the Program

The book is set out systematically with each step providing exercise to follow, tasks to complete and techniques to practise.

Step 1: Understanding and Improving Your Motivation to Stop or Reduce your Gambling; Establishing Outcome Goals

In Step 1 you will evaluate why you are setting out to overcome your problem gambling. This is to make sure that your motivation is governed by the right reasons, that is, that you are embarking on this self-help program for your own benefit and not to please others. It is essential that your motivation stems personally from within and that you are fully committed to change.

Step 2: Monitoring Your Level of Gambling

Step 2 outlines a way in which you can record how much gambling takes place daily. The purpose of this step is to enable you to realize exactly how much time and money you spend gambling and to identify links between emotions and cues in your environment that trigger your urge. A review of monitoring sheets at regular intervals helps plot your progress and show you how much you have achieved over time. This can encourage you to keep going during shaky times.

Step 3: Learning a Relaxation-based Skill to Enable You to Overcome the Urge to Gamble; Learning to Identify Triggers and Situations that Trigger Lapses

A practical skill with which you can counter urges as soon as

101

they appear is taught in Step 3. This is a powerful procedure which lowers the drive to gamble to a manageable level. Understanding the types of stresses and cues in the environment that remind you of gambling and learning how to tackle the tension and excitement generated by them can build your self-esteem and confidence. Instead of becoming physically tense or excited when thoughts of gambling enter your mind, with the relaxation procedure you can foster a sense of calm and control.

Step 4: Identifying and Challenging Irrational Thoughts and Beliefs Related to Gambling

Step 4 examines how irrational thoughts and distorted ways of thinking about gambling contribute to problem gambling behavior. There is little doubt that false beliefs about gambling being a source of income or opportunity to improve one's financial situation contribute to repeatedly bringing one back to try again. Challenging one's view about gambling, coming to understand the true reason underlying one's motivation to gamble and recognizing what the activity is really all about can radically alter one's desire to continue gambling.

Step 5: Preventing Future Episodes

Step 5 teaches strategies to use in recognizing danger signals and identifying high-risk situations. Knowing when a lapse is about to happen enables one to short-circuit the process by taking appropriate decisive action. Changing lifestyle patterns to minimize contact with cues associated with gambling and learning adequate problem-solving skills is a good way of ensuring that the positive gains achieved will be maintained.

Step 6: Eliciting Family Support

Finally, overcoming gambling is made easier when family members provide strong support and encouragement. Working in cooperation with close others is one excellent way of improving marital and family relationships, as well as a source of strength in boosting commitment to change and maintaining momentum. The trustfulness and quality of one's relationships are vastly improved as a result of open communication.

A review section is provided at the end of each step to help prompt you and to act as a reminder when you return to the self-help book for revision. It is recommended that you re-read various sections and refresh your skills as time goes on.

Some Reflections on Gambling in General

At this point it may be useful to pause and offer some comments on the general nature of gambling and the principles applied in this book. There is nothing intrinsically good or bad about gambling. The negative factors associated with gambling come from faulty practices that lead to problems in various areas of one's life. The majority of people gamble sensibly and view the activity as a form of entertainment and fun. As is frequently stated, while these people hope to win, they really expect to lose. The amount they lose is limited and well within their means. For others, however, gambling gets out of hand and problems quickly follow.

Now, while for some people the only way to recover is by complete avoidance of any gambling, for others it is perfectly possible to resume the activity at controlled levels. It is important to understand that what works for one person is ineffective for another. So you must choose what you personally want to achieve from this self-help book in terms of abstinence or controlled gambling. But take care when considering this that you are not merely deluding yourself into thinking you can continue controlled gambling when it is apparent that you will only repeat a previous cycle of failed attempts.

While many suggestions offered can be of benefit, do not think that everything contained in this book will work for you, or you may be disappointed. Pick out and practise those that produce results for you.

One final word. There may be others among your friends or colleagues who you may come to consider suffer from a similar condition of problem gambling. Resist the temptation constantly to badger them to do something about their problem or to parade your successes in overcoming problem gambling. Rather, gently offer them support and encouragement by informing them of resources such as this self-help book to which they can turn for assistance. Give them time and space to come to terms with their need to seek help.

'I cannot begin to tell you how my life has changed for the better. I am no longer obsessed with thoughts of where my next pound will come from, plagued by fears that my boss will find out how much time from work I have lost, or worrying about my wife's reaction when she finds out once again I haven't paid the bills. Now, whenever I have the urge which is rare these days, I just take two minutes time out, relax and imagine myself walking away without having given in. If the urge persists, I think of how I am going to feel after I finish betting and coming out a loser. The operators are the only real winners in this game. That really turns me off gambling. The best thing about it is that for the first time in a long while, I have money in my pocket to spend on my wife and family. You should see the look on my kid's face when I come home with a present or tell him we're going out to the movies and for dinner. For once I have respect for myself. And so does my wife. Gee, it makes me feel like I'm floating on cloud nine. I should have come to my senses and stopped gambling ages ago.' Alan

Keep in mind the many benefits awaiting you from overcoming problem gambling. While you are making this decision for yourself, your partner, family and others you care about will also reap the rewards of your effort. The path to recovery is not always smooth, nor is progress along it as quick as you may expect. You must not be surprised to experience temporary setbacks on the way. However much you may feel like throwing in the towel on these occasions, it is important not to become despondent. Rather, turn them around so that you use them as an exercise in learning to help you deal more effectively with similar events in the future. A positive attitude and consistent effort will eventually pay dividends. Look forward to an improved quality of life and the enhanced self-esteem that overcoming your gambling problem will produce for you.

STEP 1

Working Out Your Motivation to Stop

' I, the State Coroner, have investigated the death of Mr M.S. On Monday 18 June, 1994 the deceased was found in his motor vehicle at the local primary school. Attached to the exhaust pipe of the vehicle was a hose that led to the interior. The investigation reveals that the deceased was a compulsive and obsessive gambler and as a result was suffering financial and marital problems. On April 4 of the same year, the deceased attempted suicide by taking an overdose. The deceased was in an emotional and unstable state but refused to seek counselling for his problems.'
(Victorian State Coroner, Australia, 1995)

Why was Mr M.S. not motivated to overcome his gambling problem?

Not everyone is prepared or ready to undergo a major change such as giving up gambling. Willingness to do so is based on individual beliefs, attitudes and prior experiences. Two psychologists, James Prochaska and Carl DiClemente, have offered a useful framework for people to determine their position on a spectrum of readiness for change.

No awareness or reluctance to acknowledge the problem.
(Denial leading to a lack of motivation to change.)

↓

Thinking about changing.
(Recognizing a problem but still not actively motivated to change.)

↓

Becoming determined to change.
(Gaining motivation and strength actually to do something to change.)
↓
Taking active steps to start changing.
(Motivated to commence actively changing.)
↓
Maintaining changes once they are made.
(Motivated to continue changes made.)

To begin with, no one can stop you from gambling. No change will occur if you choose to deny that a problem with gambling exists or if you pretend it does just to please others. Gaining motivation to change is the crucial first step toward recovery.

The desire to improve yourself must come from within, so it is important for you to understand the reasons why you are trying to give up gambling. If you are committed to improve for your own sake, then you will achieve your goals. If you are ambivalent, that is, you feel others are forcing you to give up but you would rather keep gambling given the opportunity, you are less likely to stop. However, if this is your situation, don't turn away from the possibility of improvement straight away; many gamblers have made great progress from apparently unpromising beginnings.

Even though excessive gambling causes personal distress, we know that many gamblers do not voluntarily seek help. In fact, most are pushed into it by people who are concerned by their self-destructive behavior. Not surprisingly, a move to seek help is usually triggered by a major crisis caused by gambling. The crisis may be financial, when the expenses of daily living cannot be met, there is no money left to pay the rent or creditors are constantly calling for repayments on loans. Or it may involve problems within a relationship: there may be a threat of divorce because too much time is spent away from home or there is never enough money for the children or family/partnership activities. There may be legal reasons, as when a solicitor has advised therapy to give a good impression to magistrates before being sentenced for a gambling-related crime; or an employer may have suggested it because of poor work performance.

We have treated gamblers who are clearly not motivated but are undergoing therapy to satisfy the demands of their spouses. During treatment, and for reasons we do not understand, attitudes suddenly change in a positive direction. The principle should be, then, that even if on the surface the gambler does not seem motivated to change, treatment should be encouraged. So even an unmotivated gambler may benefit from reading this self-help guide!

Generally, however, any ambivalence on your part will lead to poor compliance with instructions and resistance to therapy. It is a fundamental understanding in clinical psychology and psychiatry that people do not change behavior unless they are fully motivated. If coerced into therapy, there is a risk that you will simply go 'through the motions' of following instructions just to please others. The outcome will be that you will give the impression of doing well when in fact the problem is continuing behind people's back – and your own.

There is no benefit in fooling yourself in thinking that you really want to stop when you don't. You will deny that you have any urge to gamble or that you have placed any bets. This will lull others into a false sense of security until they discover evidence of your gambling. Then, once again, you will have undermined people's trust in you.

Understanding Your Motivation

So how do you know when you are genuine in wishing to stop your problem gambling? What causes you to become motivated to seek treatment? It may be the realization that you have hit 'rock bottom' and therefore need to change dramatically to save your marriage, coming close to suicide, public disclosure that finally lifts a 'weight off your shoulder'; or you may have just become sick of a behavior that constantly causes stress.

The first step you need to take is to be open and honest with yourself. To do this, it is very helpful to make a list of the reasons why you feel you should give up gambling. For example:

- I am always struggling to keep up with payments for the home.
- I never spend any time with my wife and children.
- I am always lying to cover up.
- I never have enough money to buy things for my family or myself.

Write down up to ten main reasons why you should stop gambling. Now rank them on a ten-point scale according to how important they are for you. Give the most important a rating of 1 and the least important a rating of 10.

Reason   Ranking

1 _____   _____

2 _____   _____

3 _____   _____

4 _____   _____

5 _____   _____

6 _____   _____

7 _____   _____

8 _____   _____

9 _____   _____

10 _____   _____

Now compare these with any arguments you can think of as to why you should continue. Write down ten reasons in favour of why you think you should continue gambling.

For example:

- I believe I can win enough money to cover all my debts.
- I get a real sense of enjoyment out of gambling.

- Gambling is a way of escaping from my worries and problems.

As in the exercise before, rank them on a ten-point scale according to how important they are for you. Give the most important a rating of 1 and the least important a rating of 10.

Reason   Ranking

1 _____ _____

2 _____ _____

3 _____ _____

4 _____ _____

5 _____ _____

6 _____ _____

7 _____ _____

8 _____ _____

9 _____ _____

10 _____ _____

Now take a few minutes to compare the two lists. Are most of the reasons given for continuing to gamble based on your desire to satisfy your own needs over and above anyone else's? As an exercise, recall the last time you won some money. Were you keen to put the cash aside so that you could gamble again the next day or did you immediately pay some outstanding bills? Now reverse the situation. When it comes to your partner putting money aside or buying personal items for her/himself, is your reaction different? Do you feel irritated and angry because you now have to spend your gambling kitty on rent or food? I'm sure you would agree that most problem gamblers like yourself keep the money for themselves and selfishly feel extremely resentful if they have to spend it on essential domestic purchases.

People who are highly motivated to overcome their gambling want to stop because:

- they have come to realize their behavior is affecting not only themselves but also those who are close to them;
- gambling is causing major problems in all aspects of their life;
- they recognize that their desire to gamble is entirely for selfish reasons;
- life would be less emotionally draining once they stopped gambling.

The Goal: Abstinence or Controlled Gambling?

A good way of testing your motivation is to consider what your overall aim is from this self-help book. Are you aiming to remain abstinent from gambling or do you wish to pursue controlled gambling?

Abstinence means that you will not gamble in any form, even soft forms such as raffles or office sweepstakes. Controlled gambling means that you will set limits on the amount and time you spend gambling each week. For example, you may set the limit at five pounds a week. Any wins are not re-gambled during the week but are put aside into a separate account. If you lose your five pounds early in the week, you do not take out any more money. You have to wait until your next allocation at the start of the next week. In this way, your maximum bet can only be five pounds over any week, irrespective of how much you are ahead.

Tick the box which best describes your self-help aim:

	Yes	No
Abstinence	☐	☐
Controlled gambling	☐	☐

If you have chosen controlled gambling, you will need to specify how much time and money you can afford each week:

Amount of money per week _____ pounds

Amount of time per week _____ hours

If you chose controlled gambling, seriously reconsider your motivation to overcome your problem gambling. Controlled gambling is an attractive aim; it allows you to justify continued indulgence in gambling while simultaneously reducing the pressure being placed on you by others to stop altogether. While it is true that a proportion of people can resume controlled gambling, we are still unable to predict with any degree of accuracy for whom this solution will work and for whom it will not.

Controlled gambling is hard to maintain because of the ease with which loss of control can occur. Frequent exposure to gambling cues, occasional wins and external stresses are all factors that act to apply pressure on you to escalate your level of involvement. The probability is that in a matter of time you will resume problem gambling habits again.

Take the example of Annabelle, a 45-year-old single mother living with a long-term partner.

'I went to the club by myself to play the slot machines. I told myself that I would only spend the ten pounds which was my weekly gambling kitty. After a short while, I had the machine up to seventy-five pounds credit, but I wouldn't take the money out. Thought of what I would do with the money, buy Christmas presents. Blew the lot, I did. Feel sick now, depressed, disgusted with myself. I would have won a hundred pounds, was only at the club for an hour and a half. Walked out convinced I would never gamble again. In a bad mood all day. I'm not meant to have money, I run around all week with nothing in my purse. Imagine, I could have walked out with a hundred pounds, now nothing again. Why do I do this?'

Two days later, Annabelle returned.

'My downfall was thinking I could win back that hundred pounds. Blew all my money. Came home, gorged myself with

112

food and felt worthless. Depressed and feeling very sick, physically and mentally. Where will I get the money to live on for the rest of the week? Gee, the only thing left to do is to borrow money from Jack and see if my luck changes. Can I really afford to stop now?'

She was back on the merry-go-round of chasing losses.

In psychological treatment programs, health professionals may recommend controlled gambling for those gamblers who refuse therapy because they do not want to give up totally or would refuse therapy because they believed it impossible to stop totally. It is considered important to encourage these people to start therapy whatever the aim. With assistance and the benefit of their own experience over time, they can come round toward more realistic expectations.

If you have selected controlled gambling as your goal at this point, it is essential that you involve your partner, friend or boss as a supervisor, that is, someone to whom you report. His/her role will be to monitor your level of gambling each week. It is also advisable to consult a health professional who will act as an additional external supervisor.

If you want to pursue controlled gambling but are reluctant to be monitored by a supervisor, then you need to review your motivation. To argue that you can monitor progress on your own without the need to be under surveillance is to show misplaced confidence or – more probably – a wish to avoid responsibility. Go back to the beginning of Step 1 and re-evaluate your motivation.

Remember, the crucial step in gaining the most from this self-help book is fully to understand your motivation. If you are uncertain, discuss the matter with your local counsellor or psychologist.

Others Motivating a Gambler to Seek Help

What should a partner do with a gambler who is reluctant to receive help? There is no one answer, but a number of suggestions can be offered as a guide:

- Resist constant nagging to go for help. Nagging raises tension and causes the gambler to dig his/her heels in refusing.
- Refrain from making appointments on behalf of the gambler with health professionals. This is his/her responsibility. Gamblers seek the easy way out and given the chance will throw responsibility for action on to others.
- Provide written material informing him or her as to what help is available and where.
- Take steps to protect yourself from any debts that the gambler may incur. Seek legal advice in respect of joint accounts.
- Take steps to distance yourself from any responsibility for the gambler's debts. You may need to obtain legal advice.
- Avoid conspiring with the gambler to keep the gambling problem hidden from family members or others. Talk about the problem freely. In this way you will gain understanding, support and advice.
- *Do not* pay any outstanding debts that the gambler may have. Again, this just makes it easy for the gambler to shirk responsibility and avoid confronting and dealing with problems that he/she has generated. Ask yourself: why should someone give up gambling if other people pay their debts? This can of course be difficult, especially if you are a parent dealing with a gambler son or daughter. It is hard to see them suffer, risk legal action and/or jeopardize their future credit ratings. However, a balance must be achieved between these types of problem and the longer-term consequences of continued excessive gambling. The aim of all this is to teach the gambler to be responsible for any problems caused by gambling and that it is up to him/her and not others to fix any damage.
- Do not treat or regard the gambler as someone who is suffering a disease over which he/she has no control. Some gamblers use the ploy of arguing that they failed in their efforts to stop gambling simply because they were ill. Blaming an illness for their behavior is totally unacceptable. Pathological gambling is not an illness defined by an *inability* to control behavior but is rather a *failure* to control

114

behavior. Gamblers fail to control themselves rather than being unable to do so.

Review of Step 1

Understanding the true reasons why you are attempting to overcome your problem gambling is essential for success. Only by being motivated for the right reasons will you continue to push yourself during periods of difficulty and remain faithful to the program. Ask yourself the following questions:

- Are you doing this for your own benefit?
- Have you written down the benefits for your family and yourself of overcoming problem gambling?
- Are you realistic in pursuing the goal of controlled gambling?
- What alternative steps have you considered if experience shows you are not capable of handling controlled gambling?

Having determined your level of motivation, in Step 2 we can proceed to track and examine more closely the actual level of your gambling activity.

STEP 2

Monitoring Your Gambling

It is all too easy to convince yourself that you do not spend too much money gambling. Research has shown that most people tend to remember wins easily and to forget losses quickly. This bias in memory leads to the false perception that you are winning more than you lose. How often have you boasted that you won, say, fifty pounds, conveniently ignoring the fact that you spent and lost seventy pounds trying to win that amount?

There are a number of reasons why monitoring your gambling is a useful strategy in overcoming your gambling.

- Keeping a record of your activities will force you to become aware of exactly how much money you are actually gambling.
- You will be able to keep track of changes in your level of gambling as you follow the instructions in this self-help book. Your motivation will increase greatly once you see improvement happening.
- Detailed records will reveal particular patterns in your gambling, for example, regularly gambling after work, in response to stress or when you are depressed. Knowing the pattern of your habit will allow you to reorganize your schedule or take alternative strategies to deal with high-risk situations.

Monitoring requires effort and consistency. At times it may feel tedious and too bothersome, and is often avoided with the excuse that there was no paper or pen handy. However, do not

116

underestimate the importance of monitoring, particularly as a useful means of picking up possible slips early on and so preventing them from developing into a relapse. If you are going to succeed, you must know how you are progressing over time. Once monitoring becomes a routine part of your practice, you will find it an invaluable tool for motivating you to keep up your efforts.

A Structured Guide for Monitoring

The key here is to record your gambling activity each day on a standard monitoring sheet. This section sets out a good example of such a sheet and offers guidelines on how best to record useful information on it.

Before we examine the recording process in detail, it is worth noting a few points that will make it easier for you to monitor your behavior.

- Prepare enough standard monitoring sheets for daily use.
- Use a separate sheet for each day.
- Make sure that you do not forget to take your daily monitoring sheet when you leave home.
- Keep all the completed sheets together in one folder.
- Record your gambling transactions immediately; do not rely on memory at the end of the day.
- You will need to record not only the actual transactions, but also your thoughts and feelings before each gambling session, and after learning the result of each bet. This will make it easier for you to identify patterns in your behavior.

A good example of a completed monitoring sheet is provided in Figure 1. (Blank sheets for your use are provided at the end of the book.) This uses horse-racing as the betting medium; of course, substitute your own form of gambling, for example, lotteries, fruit machines, where appropriate.

In column 1, simply record the time and the specific place where you gambled. This will be helpful, as we shall see shortly, in making a list of high-risk situations to avoid.

Date: _____

Day: _____

1	2	3	4	5	6	7	8
Time & place	Feelings and thoughts before gambling (rating of tension on ten-point scale – 1= low, 10 = high)	Borrowings	Cash at start of session	Cash at end of session	Win	Loss	Feelings associated with results (rating of tension on ten-point scale – 1 = low, 10 = high)
1.20 p.m. Betting shop near work.	Stressful day, worried about bills to pay. Can I win some money? (7)		45	10		35	Angry, more depressed. Worried where I will get more money from. (8)
2.20 p.m. Betting shop near work.	Form guide. Saw favourite horse at good odds. (1)		10	85	75		Happy, I'm on a roll. Another win will see me out of trouble. (1)
4.30 p.m. Betting shop near home.	Talked to a friend. Given tip for horse. Confident that I can win enough now to pay off all outstanding debts. The chance I have been waiting for. Borrow 20 pounds. (1)	20 From David, work mate. Now owe him 50 in total (but will be able to repay after winning).	85	0		95	Depressed. Kicking myself at losing money I couldn't afford. (10)
Total wins/losses & borrowings		20			75	130	Loss: 75–130 = –55 Borrowing: = 20

In column 2, describe in detail all thoughts you may have had leading to your decision to gamble. This task is not as easy as it sounds and requires a lot of practice. Spend time trying to be as precise as possible and do not be satisfied with general statements. For example, you may be feeling upset. Think of what has upset you: was it a critical remark made by your boss, did you have an argument with your wife, are you worried about some outstanding bills to pay? Did you think gambling would help you forget about your worries, discharge some of your anger and tension, or were you desperate to get the money and convinced that this was the only way to get it quickly and easily? What was the effect of these thoughts on your feelings?

Were you depressed, highly anxious and agitated, worried sick or a combination of all of these emotions? It is sufficient to make notes in point form rather than sentences if you wish, but it is important to capture the very essence of your thoughts and feelings.

Now take a few moments to rate your level of tension. Use a ten-point scale where a rating of 1 represents no tension present, and a rating of 10 indicates very high tension or anxiety. You do not have to limit yourself to rating tension. If you wish, you can substitute depression for tension. Or better still, add another rating scale to cover emotions such as anger, hopelessness and low self-esteem.

The next column, column 3, is reserved for recording any money borrowed to gamble, irrespective of its source. State the amount borrowed and from whom, and keep a running total of how much you owe that person or financial institution altogether. It's not pleasant to be reminded of your debts, but confronting them will make you realize just how much debt you are building up. A loan of twenty pounds may not seem much until you recall the fact that you already owe a substantial amount to that person; this may cause you to think twice.

A word of caution. Many people panic because of their debt and believe that their only chance of reducing it is by further gambling. When they become aware of the full extent of their debt, judgment is clouded by anxiety, heightening the urge to gamble. Remember: *gambling led you into debt; gambling will NOT lead you out of it*.

At the conclusion of each sheet's recordings, add the total for this column to see how much borrowed money you are prepared to risk.

Column 4 is designed to keep track of the amount of your own money spent on gambling. Record only the cash in hand, excluding borrowings. Money withdrawn from savings accounts or redirected from other purposes such as rent or bills should be listed in the 'Borrowings' column. We are interested only in the disposable or 'spare' cash physically in your possession. Winnings from previous bets or earlier sessions can be included. This information is useful for fully appreciating the amount turned over by you in a period of time – money that could be more productively spent. In the sample in Figure 1, the turnover is 45 + 10 + 75 = 130.

For Column 5, record the cash remaining, if any, at the conclusion of the gambling session.

The whole purpose of gambling, some think, is to win money. Columns 6 and 7, recording winnings and losses on each bet, will help quickly to dispel this myth. Simply subtract the total in column 7 from that in column 6 (in the sample, 75 - 130 = –55). The difference between these two figures gives your position at the end of the day. If the figure is a negative one, it means you have lost. I suspect that you will find that, more often than not, the figure will be negative.

Finally, in column 8, you need to record your thoughts and feelings at the end of the session. As before, rate your emotions on the ten-point scale. In the example, you are rating tension, but again you are free to change this to depression or any other feeling you wish to monitor. Remember, it is helpful to write down more than just a description, say, for example, 'depressed'. Specify *why* you are depressed, for example: 'I have let myself down again, I'm just a hopeless case.'

You will need to keep details of the final figure from your calculation of columns 6 and 7 on each sheet as a record of your progress. To do this you will need to use a separate sheet to record wins and losses from each daily completed monitoring sheet. For example, let us say that the sheet in Figure 1 records the first day's gambling in a particular week. We are interested in seeing how much you won or lost at the end of the week by keeping a running summary of your daily activities over a seven-day period, as shown opposite.

You won 103 pounds but also lost 208 pounds giving you an overall loss for that week of 105 pounds.

Reviewing Your Progress

Once you have completed monitoring your gambling activity over a week, you should review your progress in detail. This exercise will enable you to chart changes over time and will provide valuable information for you to work out what triggers your urges and causes you to lose control. Reviewing your comments about your emotions and the ratings given for each day will allow you to see any patterns in your behavior. Once you have established the links between external stresses, your thoughts and emotions and attitudes toward gambling, and application of the techniques to be described in this self-help book, you will be well on the way to overcoming problem gambling.

Running total of wins and losses

Date	Wins	Losses
Day 1		55
Day 2	24	
Day 3		56
Day 4	67	
Day 5		23
Day 6	12	
Day 7		74
Total	103	208

Here are some useful questions to ask when you come to study your monitoring sheets:

- Are there particular times when I am most likely to gamble?
- Are there specific stresses or emotions that trigger my urge at these times?
- Does the urge start after I have discussed gambling topics with friends or heard reference to gambling on the television or radio?
- Is there a regular venue I go to gamble and feel comfortable?
- Is there a consistent pattern of emotions associated with winning?
- What about losing? What are my most likely reactions after a loss?

- Does the rate of gambling increase when I am upset? Do I binge when down?

Let us review our example above. In column 2, it is clear that the trigger for gambling is worry associated with not having money to pay bills. Your level of tension is already high, but increases after losing. Tension drops dramatically when you are confident of winning and have won, and continues to be low as your confidence is raised again. But after you have lost at the end of the day's gambling, your tension is rated at the maximum, and you are also depressed.

Now that you are aware of this pattern, you can take steps to dampen your unrealistic enthusiasm when you are given a tip or following a win. Write down on a small index card the following phrase:

'Even though I am happy and confident now, how will I feel WHEN I LOSE?'

Place this card in your wallet or purse where you hide your gambling money. Read it every time you have the urge to gamble. Basically, you know that eventually you *will lose* gambling. You have proved this to yourself ever since you have started gambling; otherwise you would not be where you are today.

The practical advantage of understanding the emotions and situations that trigger your gambling is that you will be ideally placed to apply the cognitive behavioral techniques outlined in the following steps. Therefore you must not cut corners when you monitor. Resist the temptation to think that you know your own habits; many people are surprised to find out the difference between what they think they do and what they actually do in real life.

I cannot stress enough how important it is to keep accurate records. You should allocate a fixed time each week, when you are not rushed and have plenty of time, to go over the monitoring sheets. It is very helpful to talk to your supporting partner or health professional about what you have written.

Daily monitoring sheet

Date: _____

Day: _____

1	2	3	4	5	6	7	8
Time & place	Feelings and thoughts before gambling (rating of tension on ten-point scale – 1 = low, 10 = high)	Borrowings	Cash at start of session	Cash at end of session	Win	Loss	Feelings associated with results (rating of tension on ten-point scale – 1 = low, 10 = high)
Total wins/losses & borrowings						Wins/Loss: = Borrowing: =	

They should be able to pick up on things that you may have perhaps overlooked or give you suggestions to think about.

Monitoring Sheets for Your Use

Blank copies of the daily monitoring sheet and weekly summary sheet are provided below for your use. First, make a number of photocopies of the sheets for use over the coming weeks (some spare sheets are already provided at the end of the book). Then fill a couple in as samples, using the guidelines in the text above, to familiarize yourself with the process.

Running summary of weekly activities

Week: _____

Date: _____

Date	Wins	Losses
Day 1		
Day 2		
Day 3		
Day 4		
Day 5		
Day 6		
Day 7		
Total		

Review of Step 2

Have you made enough copies of the monitoring sheets to use over the next few weeks? It is a good idea to overestimate the number of copies needed; it is best to have spares rather than to risk running short.

Now, before moving on to the next step, make sure you are familiar with the process. Are you writing down enough information about your mood and stresses, so that when you study it you will be able to see any patterns that are present?

Noting what thoughts frequently enter your mind when you have the urge to gamble will help you later on when you try to identify the irrational thoughts and ideas about gambling that act as a fertilizer to feed your problem gambling habits.

Are you recording details immediately, when they happen, or relying on memory by writing things down at the end of the day? With problem gambling, memory is often not only inaccurate, but also biased in the way it selectively remembers certain information. There is a tendency to underestimate amounts lost and to minimize unpleasant emotions. Preferring to recall wins and positive feelings is a self-defeating strategy merely designed to justify more gambling.

Are you reviewing the monitoring sheets regularly? Do not simply glance at them, but study the relationship between various aspects of what you have recorded.

Finally, remember that it is in your own interest to be honest in your responses. Honesty reflects an attitude of commitment to help yourself. This is the very foundation of self-help.

STEP 3

Controlling Your Urge Using a Relaxation Technique

'Even though I have the greatest intention in the world to stop gambling, once I have the urge, nothing else matters. I just don't think of the consequences, of what might happen if I lose. Everything apart from the gambling is blocked out of my mind, I'm so confident that I will win. If something gets in my way and prevents me from gambling, I get frustrated and irritable. I can only think of ways in which I may be able to satisfy my urge as quickly as possible'. Allen

It is common to hear the complaint that the urge to gamble is overwhelming and beyond control. As you have no doubt learnt from your monitoring, no matter whatever the cause, the drive to gamble follows a similar pattern. First comes the trigger. This might be stress at work or home, others talking of their own gambling or references to gambling in the media. Inability to handle work or family pressures or general dissatisfaction with your life may cause you to think about gambling as a release of tension or way of escaping. Once the thought enters your mind, it becomes difficult to shake off. Fantasies of a major win and what it would do to your lifestyle enter your mind. You begin to feel confident of coming out ahead, and at the same time fearful that you may miss out on this opportunity. The confidence and the urge grow with every passing moment. Concentration is impossible as your mind becomes absorbed with the task of gambling. Physical symptoms of tension such as restlessness, short temper and racing heart are obvious signs of anticipation and excitement. This tension continues to build until such time as the urge is finally satisfied through gambling.

What happens if you try to resist the urge? Any attempt to break the sequence by not gambling is met with a rising tide of anxiety and stress. The nagging doubt that 'this time my luck has changed, I could win' plagues you. As one gambler said, 'I would just die if I missed out and my numbers came up, I can't afford to take the chance this time.' It is a catch-22 position: you'll feel bad if you gamble and bad if you don't.

Tackling the Urge to Gamble

In this section you will learn a simple but highly effective technique to reduce or eliminate the compelling urge that drives you to gamble. This technique is called 'imaginal desensitization' and has been developed and described by an Australian psychiatrist, Professor Nathaniel McConaghy. Simply put, this technique involves learning a brief muscle relaxation procedure and then imagining yourself about to gamble, but walking away from the scene without doing so while applying the relaxation technique. Used consistently, imaginal desensitization breaks the cycle between gambling and physical tension. It has been systematically evaluated by research and shown to be a valuable tool which you can easily apply to the particular setting relevant to you. Its strength lies in its ability to dampen down the tension associated with the urge to gamble, allowing you to use additional cognitive strategies that will be described in the next step.

Let us describe in more detail Professor McConaghy's model of the 'behavior completion mechanism' as it applies to gambling. This will assist you in gaining a solid understanding of when and how to use the technique. The model is shown in diagram form in Figure 2.

We start off by coming into contact with opportunities to gamble. This may be through friends or family inviting us to have fun. It is clear that the more regularly and frequently a person gambles, the more established the habit becomes. The stronger the habit, the lower is the threshold triggering the urge. It does not take much to elicit a response from someone

127

who gambles daily as compared to a person who gambles merely once a year.

Certain changes take place in the functioning of the brain once a habit is established. Without going into too much detail about these changes, it can be said that a mental model of the repeated habit is formed in our minds. This mental representation consists of all the links in a chain of behaviors that go to make up the total habit. For example, if we wish to pick up a glass and have a drink, a mental model of reaching out for a glass of water is activated in our mind. We start by moving our hand toward the glass. If our hand misses the glass, our intended action has not been completed. This causes a mild state of tension which motivates us to adjust our behavior so that it is completed satisfactorily.

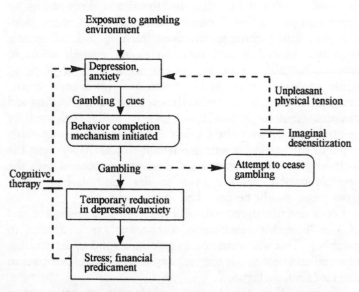

In this model, once the first link in a chain of behaviors that form a habit is activated, the whole mental model becomes activated and motivates or drives us to complete the behavior. This motivation or drive is referred to as the 'behavior completion mechanism'.

Many gamblers are aware that their compulsion arises in response to a wide range of gambling-related cues, for example, reading the form guide, lottery results, or walking past fruit machines or off-track betting offices. Though you may find it hard to believe, it is crucial to note that the compulsion is also frequently triggered by factors that do not appear to have any direct relationship with gambling, such as boredom, time of day, or apparently unrelated stresses. For example, an office worker may find his thoughts turning to gambling just before lunch-time when he often goes to the pub to play gaming machines. A housewife home alone all day may find herself anxiously waiting for everyone to leave for work or school so she can go out to play bingo; no such urge to gamble is felt on weekends when she knows everyone will be home. Typically, the urge to gamble manifests itself in response to situations of tension or stress.

Through repeated episodes we come to recognize that gambling is exciting and allows us to escape negative mood states of anxiety and depression. It is enjoyable. But gambling also results in losses which aggravate our financial stress, causing further depression and anxiety. These emotions then feed back and themselves become cues to trigger off the neuronal 'behaviour completion' model which precipitates the urge to return to gambling. As indicated in Figure 2, cognitive therapy can be used to short-circuit this pathway by providing a way to challenge distorted beliefs and teaching alternative stress management and problem-solving skills to prevent negative emotions from turning into gambling cues.

What happens if there is an attempt to prevent the habit from being carried out to completion? The neuronal model remains incomplete and a sense of unpleasant physical tension is produced. This tension persists until one finally acts out the habit completely. The reduction in tension following completion of the habit reinforces the cycle.

Imaginal desensitization works by preventing this build-up in tension and therefore its release in repeated gambling. The rehearsing of familiar gambling behavior patterns 'in imagination' while in a physically relaxed state ensures that uncontrollable levels of tension are no longer provoked by relevant cues. In this manner, the rise in tension associated with the habit not being completed is short-circuited. The drive to carry out the habit is diminished, making it easier to control the urge.

The primary purpose of imaginal desensitization is to reduce:

- the urge to gamble;
- the excitement associated with gambling;
- the persistent tension produced by attempts to resist the urge.

The benefit of imaginal desensitization is that once you have mastered it, it enables you to apply an easily learnt technique in the real-life situation as soon as the urge starts to develop.

Learning Imaginal Desensitization

Imaginal desensitization is a simple relaxation-based technique which combines physical relaxation with mental images of being confronted with an opportunity to gamble but not doing so. The instructions for the relaxation procedure and guided mental images will be recorded on an audio tape for use in each self-help session. The following summary will help you to understand the number of steps involved and how they fit together, before we move on to the actual construction of the recording.

You will need a paper and pen or pencil to write down a set of descriptions, and an audio-cassette recorder with a blank thirty-minute tape to record instructions for later use. (While it is possible for a partner or friend to read out the instructions during each session, it is usually more efficient and convenient to tape record these. This allows you to complete a session on your own whenever you have time.)

To prepare the recording:

- Write down a description of a typical example of your pattern of gambling.
- Follow the guidelines given in the section below on how to

break down your description into a series of smaller steps or scenes, and how and where to include the relaxation instructions.
- Following this pattern, read out aloud and tape record on audio cassette the description of your gambling habit, together with instructions on how to relax your muscles.
- The recorded tape is now ready for use.

Each tape recorded in this way will contain a set of instructions guiding you through a series of gambling scenes while you maintain a state of physical relaxation, passing through the following stages:

- Relaxation instructions.
- Instructions guiding you to imagine the first scene of your gambling habit.
- Relaxation instructions.
- Instructions guiding you to imagine the second scene of your gambling habit.
- Relaxation instructions.
- Instructions guiding you to imagine the third scene of your gambling habit.
- Relaxation instructions.
- Instructions guiding you to imagine the fourth scene of your gambling habit.
- Relaxation instructions.

There may be more than four scenes; four to six is usually an appropriate number.

Each recorded imaginal desensitization tape will need to be played two to three times for the first five days and then once a day until you have fully learnt the skill. After that, you may use the tape as needed.

Now let us move on to the first step in constructing the imaginal desensitization audio tapes.

Constructing a Series of Gambling Scenes

This technique requires you to provide a description of your typical gambling habits, and then to think beyond them. Recall the last three occasions when you gambled. Take a few moments to write down the sequence of events that took place on each occasion, from when you first had the urge until you actually gambled. Add to this a description of your feelings when you have lost. Now add how you would feel if you were able to anticipate these feelings *before* you gambled, and use them to deter you from gambling. In recording the sequence, describe each scene as though it were one link in a chain. Let me guide you with an example of a sequence written down by a betting-shop gambler.

Scene 1: I am at work feeling upset because my boss criticized me. My thoughts turn to the last three horse races run today. There's a good horse running, sure to win at good odds. Although I am working, I keep thinking of visiting the nearby betting shop immediately after work. I am looking at the time, a sense of urgency to finish work so I can place the bet.

Scene 2: Heading toward the betting shop. In the near distance I can see the sign and other punters entering. Approaching, walking closer and closer. Thoughts of winning this time enter my mind. A sense of confidence. I will beat the system.

Scene 3: Entering the premises. I can hear the race commentary broadcast over the radio. Other punters are studying the form guide. One or two people at the cashier's window placing bets. The atmosphere in the betting shop is stimulating. A group of people are discussing likely winners. I have the urge to fill out a betting slip.

Scene 4: I walk over to the counter, look at the form guide, work out how much cash I should bet on first past the post. I feel confident this time of picking a winner.

Scene 5: As I stand there about to fill out the betting slip, I look around at the other people in the betting shop. I begin to think of after the race, how I will feel when I lose. I remember the feeling of despair when my horse fails to come in, even at a place. Angry, I feel like kicking myself for thinking that I really could win. I usually think of what else I could have done with the cash instead of wasting it. I take a close look at the others in the betting shop. They all look like they have lost.

Scene 6: Bored. Even if I do win this time, I know that I will give it back eventually through my losses. Bored with the idea of betting, I turn around and start walking out of the betting shop. I am in control of my urge. Giving up this opportunity to gamble and deciding to return home makes me feel good.

Write down in the blank forms provided three such sequences, making sure that you have in each at least three to four scenes describing your typical behavior approaching your favourite form of gambling, followed by two or three scenes of you thinking about the unpleasant emotions following a loss and of being bored with the idea of gambling.

Sequence 1
Scene 1:
_____
_____

Scene 2:
_____
_____

Scene 3:
_____
_____

Scene 4:
_____
_____

Scene 5:
_____
_____

Scene 6:
_____
_____

Sequence 2
Scene 1:
_____
_____

Scene 2:
_____
_____

Scene 3:
_____
_____

Scene 4:
_____
_____

Scene 5:
_____
_____

Scene 6:
_____
_____

Sequence 3
Scene 1:
_____
_____

Scene 2:
_____
_____

Scene 3:
_____
_____

Scene 4:
_____
_____

Scene 5:
_____
_____

Scene 6:
_____
_____

Sequence 4
Scene 1:
_____
_____

Scene 2:
_____
_____

Scene 3:
_____
_____

Scene 4:
_____
_____

Scene 5:

_____

_____

Scene 6:

_____

_____

Relaxation Techniques

Having developed a series of typical patterns of behavior, we now need to learn a brief muscle relaxation technique. There are a number of different approaches to relaxing. The self-help book on *Overcoming Panic* in this series is a good reference and contains detailed instructions on the various relaxation techniques that are available. If you like, you may wish to purchase a commercially available relaxation tape to start with. But if you do choose a tape, for our purposes you will still need to practise without it so that you can perform the exercise easily and quickly.

The relaxation technique that we will be using here is a brief version of a progressive muscle relaxation procedure that is widely used for the management of stress and anxiety. Certain muscle groups such as those in the hands, arms, stomach and legs are systematically tensed for a few moments; then the tension is gradually released, allowing a sense of relaxation to flow through these parts of the body. To practise this technique, it is best to find a quiet time and place where you will be free from distractions and interruptions for about half an hour. Choose a comfortable couch or chair in which you can sit quietly with your eyes closed while you follow the instructions given to you on the tape.

With this 'mini version' of muscle relaxation, you will be able to train yourself to relax effectively in almost any situation where you find the gambling urge emerging.

A Practice Session of Imaginal Desensitization

The imaginal desensitization process involves imagining the gambling scenes you have recorded while at the same time applying the relaxation procedure. Each session should include three sequences, and each sequence should take five minutes to complete. This means that including the relaxation instructions, one whole session will be about thirty minutes in length.

Let us begin with a step-by-step example of a treatment session.

Preparation
- Find a quiet comfortable space where you will not be disturbed for half an hour. Sit in a relaxing chair; or you may prefer to lie down on a couch.
- Close your eyes, settle down and focus your attention on your breathing. Take a breath, hold it, and now slowly let it out saying the word 'relax'. Let go of all the tension in the muscles in your body with each slow breath out.
- Concentrate on the instructions as they are read out or played on the tape. It is important that you keep a focus on imagining the scenes being presented. Do not allow yourself to drift off or become distracted by, for example, thinking of tasks you have to do.
- Most importantly, do not drift off into sleep. This is an active technique that requires effort and attention on your part. Relaxation is not simply becoming drowsy or dozing. Proper relaxation will reduce your muscle tension, slowing down your rate of breathing and metabolism while you are still awake.
- How vividly you are able to visualize scenes is not important. Good results have been achieved with people who are poor at mental imagery. The key to success is combining the relaxation with (even weak) images of gambling.

Instructions to be Recorded on Audio-cassette Tape
We are now ready to commence tape recording a session for use. Let us start the procedure using one sequence as an example to follow.

137

The following instructions are to be read out aloud and tape recorded:

Make yourself comfortable on the chair. Close your eyes and clear your mind of any thoughts or images and focus your attention on your breathing . . . [pause] . . . Take a deep breath and let it out slowly . . . [pause] . . . Just breathing easily and gently now, no effort, breathing as you normally would. Now, as you breathe out I want you to say to yourself, 'Relax'.

Now I want you to clench your hands into fists as tightly as you can. Focus your mind on the tension building up in your hands and the rest of your body . . . [pause] . . . Hold that tension there . . . [pause] . . . notice how uncomfortable that tension feels . . . [pause] . . . holding it for a moment longer . . . [pause] . . . Now relax, let go of the muscles and allow your hands to relax, relax your hands and your arms. Allow the tension to flow out . . . [pause] . . . allow the tension to flow down your arms and out of your fingers. Clearing your mind of thoughts, focusing your attention on your hands and your arms . . . [pause] . . . allowing your hands and arms to become heavier and heavier, letting yourself become more and more relaxed, repeating the work 'relax' as you breathe out . . . [pause] . . . allowing your hands and arms to become heavier and heavier.

Now, turning your attention to your neck and shoulders, let that feeling of relaxation in your hands and your arms move up to your neck and shoulders . . . [pause] . . . letting your head fall forward as it begins to feel relaxed . . . [pause] . . . letting your shoulders go . . . [pause] . . . just feel the tension flowing down your arms out of your hands and fingers, down your body and out of your legs and feet as you are relaxing your whole body . . . [pause] . . . just continue relaxing, noticing how nice and peaceful you are beginning to feel, just letting all of the tension out . . . [pause] . . . feel it flowing down your neck and shoulders, through your arms and out of your hands and fingers, down your body into your legs and out of your feet . . . [pause] . . . your whole body becoming heavier and heavier, more and more relaxed . . . [pause] . . . slowing your thoughts down and focusing your attention on your body, allowing yourself to become heavier and heavier, becoming very relaxed . . . [pause] . . . Just continue relaxing for a while longer.

SEQUENCE 1

Scene 1: Now imagine that you are at work. It's been a bad day; your boss has criticized you over something you've done. You feel resentful and tense and want to get away from it all. As you brood over your problems, you notice the newspaper nearby and see the form guide. Suddenly you remember a good horse is running at the races and you start to think of placing a bet on it. You realize that it's not long to finishing time now. Your thoughts turn to heading off toward the betting shop straight after work . . . You feel a strong urge to go to the betting shop, you have been thinking about it for several hours. You can hardly wait until work finishes . . . [pause] . . . Looking forward to the excitement of betting. Recall how you felt in the past as you think about going to the betting shop straight after work. But as you do so, let yourself become relaxed, let the tension out of your body . . . [pause] . . . Allow yourself to become more and more relaxed with each breath out, feel the tension flow out of your body.

Recall the thoughts in your mind as you think about going to the betting shop, looking forward to backing a few horses, confident that you can win, a strong expectation that you will win this time. You feel good: thinking of betting helps you forget work problems. Also, you remember that you need to pay some bills. There is a lot of pressure on you to get some money to pay those debts. Let yourself relax as your mind focuses on this scene, feeling your muscles becoming even more relaxed, loose and floppy as you visualize this scene . . . [pause] . . . Continue relaxing . . .

You've got nothing else planned after work, you want to give yourself some time out and unwind. Recall the excitement of gambling . . . [pause] . . .

Continue to focus on letting yourself relax . . . [pause] . . .

Scene 2: You're now heading for the betting shop. You're

getting closer and closer. You can see the betting shop in the distance, the sign on the shop, the people walking in and out. Recall the feelings as you near the entrance, the anticipation, and the strong urge to go in and place some bets. Try to recall those feelings . . . [pause] . . . You're confident that you will win this time, luck's on your side . . . [pause] . . . Now is the chance that you have been waiting for.

But as you keep recalling those feelings, I want you to keep focusing on relaxing. Allow yourself to continue to relax, saying in your mind the word 'relax' as you breathe out, feeling all of the tension flowing away, out through your hands and your feet . . . [pause] . . .

Scene 3: Imagine yourself entering the betting shop, going in through the door. Now imagine yourself inside. Try to recall the excitement . . . [pause] . . . The race commentary in the background, the odds being displayed on the video screen, the television channel showing some of the races. The excitement is in the atmosphere. People milling around studying the form. You can hear them talking about which horses have the best chance. Try to visualize this scene as clearly as you can . . . [pause] . . . Try to recall the emotions and feelings you have experienced, recall the anticipation. Allow yourself to relax as much as you can while you visualize this scene, letting all the tension flow away . . . [pause] . . .

Scene 4: Imagine yourself as you walk over to the counter to look at the form, going down the list of runners. Noticing a few good bets with long odds, certain of a good return on your money. Start to think of the money that you need as you are standing there looking at the field. Feeling the anticipation rising in your body as you are standing there trying to pick a horse . . . [pause] . . . Allowing yourself to relax, focusing on your breathing, as you are concentrating on the scene in your head . . . [pause] . . .

You've read the form guide, selected the race and the horse you're going to back, and now you've checked the running time . . . [pause] . . . There are a few people ahead of you at the bench. You write out your ticket and turn to take it over to the cashier, confident you have made the right choice this time. You join the line of people waiting to place their bets . . . as you see yourself standing there allow yourself to relax, focusing on your breathing . . . [pause] . . . Let yourself become physically more and more relaxed as you visualise the scene . . . [pause] . . .

Scene 5: As you are standing there in line your thoughts turn to previous occasions, of the times when you lost and the feelings associated with losing . . . [pause] . . . You realize that you are probably not going to win this time either. You start to think of how you feel when you lose, when you are left short of money at the end of the day . . . [pause] . . . The bills that still need to be paid. You're starting to have second thoughts about spending your time and money in the betting shop. Thinking about the time you are wasting and the money you will be losing. You begin to get bored. You start looking at the people around you and you see just how bored they really look . . . [pause] . . .

Let yourself recall these thoughts now, of how disappointed you were, the feelings of remorse for having spent time and money in the betting shop. Let yourself recall these feelings now. You are finding yourself becoming increasingly bored with spending time in the betting shop, with gambling . . . [pause] . . . You start to think of other things that you could be doing, of other things you could be spending your money on. Let yourself visualize this scene in your mind . . . [pause] . . . the feelings of boredom associated with gambling . . .

As you do this, continue to let yourself relax . . . [pause] . . . Let all of the tension flow out of your muscles . . . [pause] . . .

Scene 6: As you move closer in line to the cashier you think more and more of the times when you've made the wrong choice in the past and lost. You think of all the money you've lost. You recall how miserable you felt then . . . [pause] . . . You decide not to place your bet. Instead, you crumple up the ticket and turn away.

As you turn away let yourself relax, letting all of the tension flow away . . . [pause] . . . You're feeling heavier and heavier as your muscles go loose and floppy.

Now imagine yourself as you decide to walk out of the betting shop, deciding not to gamble, feeling relaxed and at ease with yourself . . . [pause] . . . You've decided to pass up this opportunity to gamble, feeling quite relaxed as you walk out, you still have your money . . . You leave the noise of the betting shop and walk outside, thinking of other things you could be doing with your time. You feel relaxed and in control, pleased with yourself and your decision . . . [pause] . . . quite content and relaxed having walked out of the betting shop, feeling good that you have decided not to gamble, happy with yourself . . . [pause] . . .

As you do this, let yourself continue to relax, letting all of the tension flow away, feeling heavier and heavier as your muscles go loose and floppy . . . [pause] . . .

Giving up this opportunity to gamble, deciding to go home, feeling quite good, feeling in control of your urges, feeling satisfied with the decision you have made . . . [pause] . . .

Keep visualizing this scene as you allow yourself to continue to relax as much as you can.

Closing instructions for Sequence 1: Now clear your mind of all thoughts and allow yourself to relax . . . [pause] . . . Put all other thoughts out of your mind and focus attention back on to your body, letting yourself relax . . . [pause] . . . becoming more and more relaxed, sinking down into the chair. Just continue relaxing now for a few minutes . . . [pause] . . . Letting the tension flow out of your body, becoming more and more relaxed. Enjoy that feeling . . . [pause] . . . Keep relaxing and focusing your attention on your body. Let all other thoughts out of your mind.

Now follow the relaxation instructions given at the start of the session for the next two to three minutes.

Then continue with the next sequence. Repeat exactly the same set of instructions as above, but substitute the set of gambling-related scenes you wrote down for your second sequence. Then go through the process with each of the other sequences.

Remember, each of the sequences is made up of three to four gambling-related scenes followed by two or three scenes related to boredom and the unpleasant feelings you experience after a loss. Three or four sequences together make up a full session lasting about twenty minutes.

After you have completed the third or fourth sequence, read out the closing instructions for the session:

Closing instructions: Allow any tension to flow out of your body as you visualize this scene ... [pause] ... letting yourself become more and more relaxed as you do so. Continue relaxing as you let the tension out. Now, clear your mind of all your thoughts. Just focusing on your body ... [pause] ... letting all of the tension out and letting yourself become more and more relaxed, enjoying that peaceful sensation of relaxation ... [pause] ... Just continue relaxing now for a few minutes longer. When you decide to get up, open your eyes slowly, stretch your muscles and slowly rise.

You have now successfully completed the tape recording of the session.

Effects of Imaginal Desensitization

What effects can you expect once you have mastered the technique? Do not expect immediate noticeable changes. The effect of this therapy will become obvious over time, often a week or two after you have completed ten to fifteen sessions. Then you will notice that the drive to gamble is absent or so weak that you can easily control it.

'After I had finished ten sessions I didn't think the technique worked. There was no difference in how I felt. But a strange thing happened as time went on. I noticed that I wasn't rushing to open the form guide and when I did, there was no feeling of excitement left. It really struck me one day after work. My usual routine was to drop into the betting shop on my way home. But on this day, I actually forgot to walk in and went straight past it. I was surprised because it was only when I reached my front door that I realized I had walked straight past the shop without one thought of going in. My self-confidence has risen because I feel more able to control my urge when I am exposed to gambling situations. I can best describe the change as now being bored with the idea of gambling.' Andrew (age 35 years)

Recommended Timetable and Additional Hints

To make it easier to learn and apply the technique, try the following suggestions:

- For each sequence, write down each scene immediately followed by the relaxation instructions, as we have done in the above example.
- Repeat this step for each of the sequences you are going to use.
- Tape record each session on an audio-cassette recorder. Read out the instructions aloud, slowly, with a pause between the sentences in each scene. Do not rush; give yourself sufficient time to imagine the scene and to relax adequately.
- Each scene should take about five minutes to complete, so take your time.
- Wait two or three minutes before proceeding to the next scene and relax during this time.

Now you are ready to train yourself in the technique. Practice is crucial; the more you practise, the more skilled you will become in applying the technique efficiently. To gain maximum benefit you should do two to three thirty-minute sessions each day for five days: that is, a minimum of ten sessions over one week. Allow two to three hours between each session. This has been shown to be the most effective schedule. After this you may use the tape as necessary as a booster session whenever the need arises.

Once you have clearly mastered the technique, you will be

able to put it into practice automatically whenever you experience an urge coming on. Do not become complacent. Continually apply the technique whenever you have an urge, no matter how small it may seem. Complacency is likely to result in a return of the drive to gamble.

A number of sensible gamblers have recommended the use of portable 'Walkman'-type cassette players with earphones when they are away from home as a very helpful strategy. This is a good idea and worth using.

Review of Step 3

The relaxation procedure described in this step is a highly effective way of controlling your urge to gamble. You must use it whenever you experience an urge to gamble, no matter how small that urge feels.

It is best to tape record the instructions and use the audio cassette each time you practise. Alternatively, have someone supervise each session by reading out instructions to you.

Are you falling asleep or becoming distracted during sessions? If so, practise when you are not tired or sleepy. Make a special effort to focus on the instructions given to you. The more effort you put into learning the technique, the greater will be your reward.

Once you have completed at least ten to fourteen sessions over a week using the audio tape, you should be so familiar with the technique that you can do it on your own. Ideally, with practice you will be able to relax and apply the technique in less than three or four minutes. Then you can practise when you are travelling to work and in your lunch break. All you require is a few minutes of uninterrupted time.

Most importantly, are you learning to relax and visualize the scenes in real situations where you are exposed to gambling-related cues? This is a practical skill that you must put into effect when you are confronted with any cue that triggers off your gambling urge.

Controlling Gambling-related Cues

In Step 3, you learnt a relaxation procedure to use whenever an urge to gamble appeared at any stage. It should come as no surprise that a wide variety of cues associated with gambling, such as hearing friends talking about a hot favourite at the track, watching the lottery draw on television or walking past a betting office, can act as a trigger to set off that urge. Why is this so? Well, anticipation of winning money creates a sense of pleasure or excitement, that is, a positive feeling of physical arousal. This feeling is so strong at times that some gamblers describe it as being similar to a drug 'high'. Any cue or behavior that occurs immediately beforehand is also likely to become associated with the excitement. This is called conditioning. These cues quickly become a signal activating gambling-related thoughts and feelings.

Physical Environments as a Trigger for Gambling

You may be surprised to learn that in addition to cues directly related to gambling, places, times and even emotions can also act as triggers. When you regularly visit the fruit machines during the lunch break, go to the betting office on Saturday afternoon or read the form guide over breakfast, a regular pattern develops. Your excitement in anticipation of gambling becomes associated with these specific times. Later on, these times themselves turn into signals reminding you of gambling. A good example is that of hunger. Many people eat meals at regular times. When you notice the time an hour or so before your usual mealtime, you feel hunger because you know that it is time to eat soon, even though your body is not really starved. On the other hand, if you are busy and distracted and lose your sense of time, you do not feel any hunger until you next notice the time or when your body is really starved of nutrition.

When reviewing your monitoring sheets, look for any link between physical settings and your urge to gamble. Common settings that may act as triggers are:

- reading the form guide in the newspaper;
- seeing an amusement arcade while walking down the street;
- watching a television broadcast of the lottery draw;
- going out to lunch at the local which is near the amusement arcade;
- buying the Saturday morning paper;
- discussing race results with friends over a drink;
- listening to race/lottery results on the radio;
- being on the way home after work;
- noticing a betting office as you walk/drive by.

These are called 'situational cues'.

Write down the common situational cues that lead you to increase your gambling urge.

1 _____

2 _____

3 _____

4 _____

5 _____

6 _____

7 _____

8 _____

9 _____

10 _____

Hints on Handling Situational Cues

An effective way of controlling your urge is to avoid any situation or activity that serves to remind you of gambling. This is easier said than done; after all, there are reminders of gambling almost everywhere we go, in advertising, media reports on winners, local betting shops and outlets and discussions among friends. While you may not realistically be able to avoid every cue, there are ways of minimizing your exposure to them.

Try some of the following.

- Deliberately avoid reading the paper's sports section containing the race results. Ask your partner to remove these before you start reading. Once you lose contact with the form, your interest will gradually diminish.
- Turn off the television or radio when results are being broadcast. Do not listen and, more importantly, do not play mental games of picking the results to see how you would have done had you placed a bet. This is definitely to be avoided as it serves only to fuel your interest.
- When friends invite you to play the slot machines during the lunch break, politely decline. Suggest some alternative activity, for example, having a chat at a coffee shop or window shopping. Do not go with the intention of only watching. All that will happen is that your urge to join in will rise, especially if you see someone win. An excuse frequently made is that you will lose friends if you don't join in. But ask yourself, what is more important to you, socializing with these people or overcoming your gambling? The choice is yours. If these friends are close to you, let them know of the difficulty you have controlling your gambling. Ask for their cooperation in helping you. If they are true friends, they will go out of their way to help by not talking about gambling in your presence or inviting you to come gambling with them. If they do not respond, then ask yourself, are these true friends that are worth keeping? If gambling is the only bond holding you and these friends

together, I would have serious reservations about the quality of the relationships.

- If you gamble regularly on the way home, take a different route or offer someone a lift home. Having someone else present will make you think twice because of the need to explain where you are going.
- Arrange alternative activities with your family or friends during high-risk times. For example, invite friends over at weekends or organize an outing with family at times when you would normally gamble. Often the urge to gamble fades once you realize that there is no possibility of gambling because of other commitments.
- As you come into contact with a cue that sets off thoughts of gambling in your mind, apply the relaxation technique you have learnt. Take a deep breath, hold it for a slow count to three, then let your breath out slowly, saying the word 'relax' as you do so. Start your muscle relaxation by clenching your fists and then relaxing your whole body as you slowly let the tension out. Begin the imagery with the scenes you have learnt.
- Bring to mind the four most negative consequences you can think of should you act on your urge, gamble and lose. Do not fantasize about winning; you know from experience that you will most likely lose – if not on this next occasion, then certainly over the next few times. Always ask yourself: 'How will I feel *when*, and not *if*, I lose?

Emotions as a Trigger for Gambling

In the field of addiction, it is well known that negative mood states of depression, anxiety and anger play a major role in causing loss of control to occur. For many people, gambling is an opportunity to escape from everyday stresses and problems surrounding them. Often you hear the gamblers say: 'I just couldn't cope, I felt so unhappy. Playing the fruit machines [betting on the horses, going to bingo] lets me forget about life altogether.' This is similar to what happens in alcohol addiction. Drinking enables the drinker to temporarily reduce their level of tension. So, whenever there is stress, the alcoholic is likely to drink. The same is true of gambling.

In these circumstances, reinforcement of gambling behavior occurs in two ways. The first is the lift in mood resulting from the excitement of anticipating a win. Winning makes you feel good, improves your self-esteem and puts you into a physical state of positive arousal. Secondly, the concentration and excitement distract you from your worries and cares. In this way, becoming totally absorbed in gambling reduces your tension by shifting your attention away from unpleasant thoughts.

A similar situation may apply with respect to anger. Following an argument, people often respond with prolonged anger, becoming uptight and brooding about things that were said to them. They feel resentful and frustrated at not being able to handle the situation or get their own way, or are devastated by criticism aimed at them. This is a most unpleasant emotional state. In many respects anger is an emotion that can be used productively if channelled properly into overcoming the sources of frustration. But unfortunately, many people tend to bottle up their anger inside instead of expressing it appropriately. The build-up in anger needs to be discharged, and gambling is one readily available channel. Ask yourself, does your urge to gamble arise immediately after an argument? Do you feel like 'taking it out' on gambling?

Look at your monitoring sheet as described in Step 2 above. Can you identify any consistent pattern linking your gambling with unpleasant mood states or anger? If so, you are now in a good position to learn alternative strategies to eliminate unpleasant negative moods. There are a number of excellent self-help books in this series aimed at overcoming depression, anxiety and low self-esteem. Consult these for useful hints on how to reduce negative moods, as well as for detailed instructions on effective problem-solving strategies which we do not have space here to examine in detail. Do not forget, too, that your local doctor or counsellor can also direct you to individual or group skills training to assist you.

Some common emotions triggering urges to gamble are:

- feelings arising from an argument at home;
- feelings arising from being criticized at work by your employer;
- stress and anxiety caused by interpersonal or work-related difficulties;
- worry about debts and/or not having enough money to pay bills;
- anxiety about people finding out how much I do actually gamble;
- fear that someone will find out about the money I stole to gamble;
- feeling generally unhappy with my life;
- anger at my partner/spouse for not paying me enough attention;
- resentment that my wife is spending all her time with the children and ignoring me;
- resentment that my husband is never at home;
- feeling a need to win the affection of my friend/partner through buying her things;
- distress that friends my age have so much more than me – car, home, stereo, etc. – and wanting to 'catch up' with them quickly.

Write down the emotions that you have noticed trigger your urge to gamble.

1 _____

2 _____

3 _____

4 _____

5 _____

6 _____

7 _____

8 _____

9 _____

10 _____

Hints on Handling Emotions: Stress Management

It is all too easy to blame loss of control on your emotions. Wendy, a twenty-five-year-old married secretary, was upset that her husband of two years was staying at work late almost every night. She felt that he was not showing interest in her and was afraid that he would have an affair. Miserable and unhappy, she would play the slot machines when she knew he would be home late. As time went on, she became angry toward him. She felt she was teaching him a lesson by losing all their savings. Part of her low self-esteem grew out of the fact that she believed that she was no longer able to control her behavior, and was at the mercy of her emotions.

In therapy, we discussed the importance of communicating her unhappiness and anger to her husband more directly and openly. She quickly realized that her husband was not aware of her feelings, let alone of her gambling. Following some joint therapy sessions, she was able to express her feelings, resulting in a change in her husband's work pattern. Her urge to gamble declined rapidly. At this point she accepted responsibility for her emotions and understood how they influenced her behavior.

Some comments on stress management skills are relevant here, because we know that stress is one element that commonly leads to impaired control over behavior. When overall stress levels are high, you may be more likely to be affected by worries over your ability to handle matters. You may be more likely to make poor decisions, which aggravate the situation. For example, inability to cope with stressful situations or anxiety often leads people to use alcohol or illicit drugs or to become dependent on anti-anxiety medication. Similarly, escape into gambling is a strategy used by some to cope with stress. However, the financial problems caused by gambling only add further to the existing stresses, resulting in a reinforced desire to escape through more gambling. And so the cycle continues.

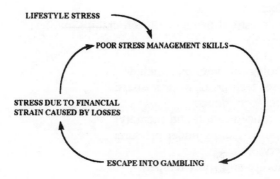

All of us experience general symptoms of stress on occasions, for example when we are confronted with pressure at work, failure to measure up to expectations, the birth of a baby or problems trying to save money for holidays or important purchases. The list of potentially stressful events is limitless; situations that some people find distressing are not at all distressing to others, and vice versa.

It is important to remember that not all stress is harmful, and most of us function better with some stress in our lives. A little anxiety before we have to take a test or give a speech may actually improve our performance as we become more alert and focused on the task. Too much stress, however, can overwhelm us. When this happens we tend to pay a lot of attention to the uncomfortable symptoms of stress rather than the task we have to do and our performance may suffer.

There are two parts to a stress response, the physical and the psychological. Some people tend to respond with physical symptoms of distress such as headaches, gastrointestinal pains or general lack of energy, while others tend to worry excessively, suffer low self-worth, feel pressured or become irritable. Review your monitoring sheets and see which type of reaction is most common for yourself.

Physical symptoms of stress include:
- muscle tension and weakness;
- increased heart rate;
- increased rapidity of breathing;
- headaches;
- gastrointestinal pains - stomach cramps, nausea;
- agitation.

Psychological symptoms include:
- sadness, feelings of worthlessness;
- low self-confidence;
- poor concentration and memory;
- constantly feeling under pressure;
- anxiety;
- irritability and short temper;
- excessive worry.

Before we consider how best to deal with excessive stress, try to pinpoint some of the sources of stress in your own life and identify why they are so stressful, using the blank list provided.

Source of stress	What makes this stressful situation so difficult to handle?
1 _____	_____
_____	_____
2 _____	_____
_____	_____
3 _____	_____
_____	_____
4 _____	_____
_____	_____
5 _____	_____
_____	_____

In reducing your overall stress levels, it is often useful to distinguish between *external* and *internal* sources of stress. External stressors are those that occur in our environment and may be beyond our immediate control. For example, criticism at work by an irritable boss, the car breaking down in heavy traffic, getting burgled or moving house are all considered to be external stressors because these events may not be under your direct control. Internal stressors, on the other hand, are those that we create for ourselves through negative attitudes, distorted thinking, poor time management and weak problem-solving skills. They may include the feelings of needing the love and approval of everyone you meet, the inability to say 'no' for fear of rejection, or the tendency to accept too many demands on your time and energy. Internal stressors are the most common sources of stress, and yet they are also the most frequently ignored or overlooked.

It is not unusual for people to experience a combination of external and internal stressors which interact with one another. For example, imagine your family wants you to take them away during the school holidays and you realize that you have hardly any savings left (external stressor). What if there is no opportunity to earn extra cash or to borrow from friends or the bank (external stressor)? What would you do? Would you start blaming yourself for being incompetent (internal stressor), working yourself up into such a state that you start thinking of any way of getting that money? Or would you try to discuss the matter with your spouse or partner to try to find a solution? Can you think of other approaches to solving the problem that do not involve turning to gambling?

People differ in the ways they cope with stress. Some coping skills, such as simply avoiding stressful situations, may be more effective in the short term than in the long term. Avoiding stressful situations by immersing yourself in gambling is a poor coping strategy as any relief gained is temporary.

In overcoming general symptoms of stress, both your physical and your psychological health need to be addressed. Because the mind and the body are so closely linked, physical ill health can result in mental ill health, and vice versa. For example, if you do not get adequate sleep or have not been maintaining a healthy diet, you may start to feel irritable or anxious. Alternatively, if you become depressed you may lose your appetite, lose weight and become run down. Conversely, many people report that they feel happier and more energized when they improve their level of fitness by undertaking a regular exercise programme. Strategies to improve your physical and mental health will be discussed in the sections that follow.

Improving Your Physical Health

The main components of a program to improve your physical health include sleep, exercise, diet and physical relaxation. If you focus on improving each of these aspects of your physical health, you will probably notice significant improvement in your ability to handle stress.

Sleep Everyone has different requirements for the amount of sleep they need. In addition, some people function better late at night, while others may find that they are most alert in the mornings. By recognizing what your normal sleep requirements are and when you are most alert, you may be able to modify your daily activities to suit your natural 'sleep–wake' body rhythm.

If sleep is a problem, try to examine critically exactly what the issues are that prevent you from getting a restful night's sleep and the strategies you may use to overcome it.

Exercise Regular exercise can not only help you to get fit, but can also be a useful way to 'work off' tension and boredom, especially if you are spending most of your day at a desk or sitting down in one spot. Participating in team sports can help you to broaden your social network, which may take your mind off your stressors and anxiety symptoms.

People who are physically fit also tend to sleep better than those who have not been getting regular exercise.

Diet A well-balanced, healthy diet is crucial to maintaining good physical and mental health. Low blood sugar levels or certain vitamin deficiencies can make you feel tired or run down and vulnerable to stress symptoms. Too much coffee, tea, 'cola' drinks or foods containing large amounts of chocolate or sugar may leave you feeling 'hyped up'.

Because nicotine (in cigarettes) is a stimulant, smoking can also increase your feelings of anxiety – apart from seriously affecting your physical health. If you are a smoker, consider cutting down or quitting as part of your overall stress management program.

Many people who suffer from anxiety report that small amounts of alcohol help them to cope, especially in social situations. Unfortunately, the regular use of alcohol to control anxiety is counterproductive in the long term as it is easy to become dependent and then to suffer from serious withdrawal symptoms. Furthermore, regular alcohol use can lead to a number of medical complications, some of which may be life-threatening.

Physical relaxation This is often a neglected area of stress management. While it is important to be concerned about getting enough sleep, exercise and healthy food, it is equally important to consider regular physical relaxation as part of an overall plan for anxiety management. Relaxing by the beach, fishing, going to the movies or getting a massage can all be useful to revitalize those tired muscles and relieve your mind of stress.

Another method of relaxing is to practise a technique known as progressive muscle relaxation. This technique helps to get rid of the daily build-up of unpleasant muscle tension. If you suffer from panic attacks, learning to slow your breathing down may also help to reduce your overall arousal level. For further guidance on dealing with panic attacks, consult the book *Overcoming Panic* in this series.

Improving Your Mental Health

The key ingredients in improving your psychological health are to learn how to become more goal-directed, to manage your time more efficiently and to solve your day-to-day problems in a systematic way. Furthermore, mental stress can often be reduced by examining how accurately you are interpreting stressful situations and by challenging any irrational negative perceptions of yourself.

Goal-setting This is a useful skill which ensures that you prioritize your tasks and acknowledge your successes when you achieve your goals. Try setting yourself small daily goals at first, then work up to the larger goals that may have been worrying you for some time.

Time management Just as important as goal-setting is being able to allocate enough time to yourself to achieve those goals. In fact, these two tasks often go hand in hand. Make sure that when you set yourself realistic goals, you have also allowed yourself enough time to achieve them.

Problem-solving Not all of us are good at problem-solving. For many of us, this is a skill that may require instruction and regular practice. Effective problem-solving involves first identifying the actual problem; then considering as many solutions as possible, no matter how strange or outrageous they seem; and then weighing up the pros and cons of each solution before selecting a particular solution or solutions to your problem.

Implementing and reviewing the outcome of your solution will help you assess whether your problem is indeed solved or whether you need to consider other related problems. Try this strategy of problem-solving first on small problems, then work up to larger ones which may be made up of several smaller worries.

Challenging and changing negative thinking styles This skill will be addressed further in later steps, and so we will only touch upon it briefly here. In essence, it involves, first, identifying any consistently negative ways in which you may be interpreting stressful situations; then actively challenging those irrational thoughts or perceptions; and finally changing these negative thoughts to positive, more appropriate perceptions which do not generate high levels of distress.

Review of Step 4

Ideally, you should avoid contact with anything to do with gambling. Of course, this is not really possible because there is so much reference to gambling in everyday life – in the media, in advertising and in topics of conversation with friends and colleagues at work and socially. Nevertheless, it is important that you reduce as far as possible any contact with cues related to gambling.

The urge to gamble can be triggered by cues in the environment (external cues) or by negative emotions and worry (internal cues). List the situations you commonly come across in your everyday activities that remind you of gambling. Write down realistic strategies that you can use to help you avoid contact with these situations. Brainstorm these strategies with your partner or others. They may offer additional suggestions that you did not think of. Plan ahead by preparing a series of steps that you may take if you suddenly find yourself confronted with a situation that is going to trigger your gambling urge. For example, how will you excuse yourself from a conversation if the topic turns to gambling? What can you say?

Identify the internal stresses that cause you to try to escape into a world of gambling. Learn to become aware of, and overcome, negative emotional states before they take hold of you. Do not cope by immersing yourself into gambling. This is an escape which will bring only temporary relief if not actually aggravate the problem. Rather, learn to tackle the source of stress using effective stress management techniques. Use relaxation methods to reduce high levels of physical tension; practise expressing your concerns to others with the aim of listening to advice on how to handle situations; improve your health by paying attention to sleep, diet, exercise and relaxation so that your physical health is strengthened. Good health is a good foundation for coping with stress.

Identifying Irrational Ideas; How to Stop Chasing Losses

Step 1 of this self-help guide started off by exploring your motivation to stop gambling. In Step 2, you learnt how to monitor your behavior to become aware of the way in which certain situations act to influence your thinking and gambling behavior. Having set the stage, you then, in Step 3, learnt a useful relaxation technique, designed to reduce your urge to gamble, which you could easily put into effect when actually confronted by cues in your environment. In Step 4 we moved on to consider the types of triggers operating in your environment and your own emotions that arouse the urge to gamble and ultimately set you on the course toward excessive gambling.

In this Step 5, we are going to examine closely your attitudes and belief structures related to various aspects of gambling and behavior: that is, what does gambling mean to you, and how does your attitude influence your behavior?

The Importance of Beliefs, Thoughts and Attitudes

Why are beliefs, thoughts and attitudes an important area to deal with? There is an approach to treatment in clinical psychology which is called 'cognitive therapy'. While there are many strands of cognitive therapy, they all operate on one fundamental premise. This is that cognitions – that is, any mental event that takes place in our minds: images, thoughts, beliefs, memories and attitudes – have a direct influence on our emotions. Superstitious behavior is a good example of how our beliefs cause us to behave in certain ways. Think back on your reactions and how you behaved when you last walked under a ladder, spilt salt or had a black cat walk in front of you. Next time you are gambling, take time to observe the people around you. Often, people playing the slot machines will touch the side of the machine, press the button a certain way or hold some item as a lucky charm. People believe that acting in this way increases their chances of winning.

As an exercise, write down here what attitudes and beliefs you hold about gambling – for instance, 'I believe it is possible to come out a winner', 'My skills at gambling are better than the average gambler's', 'Gambling is a way of making easy money'.

Personal beliefs and attitudes about gambling

1 _____

2 _____

3 _____

4 _____

5 _____

Cognitions are not isolated bits of mental activity. Rather, they interact to form a general view or 'schema' of the world, a map which you use to process all the pieces of information surrounding you and gather these into a meaningful whole. This map is then used as a guide in how you see yourself, the world around you and your future. People have a tendency to filter out from their environment what they don't want to see and focus only on what they want to see and that which is in keeping with their expectations. If you have a view of yourself as unable to control events in your life, a failure and unloved by others, you will tend to have low self-confidence and be unhappy. How we see ourselves and the world plays a powerful role in shaping our behavior.

To illustrate, let us consider two people in exactly the same situation, playing the fruit machines. One person holds a set of beliefs that he is lucky, that gambling is an easy way of earning additional income and that the only way he can impress others is by showing off success through smart cars and other fancy possessions. In contrast, the other person sees gambling as a form of entertainment, a leisure activity that he enjoys playing to pass the time. He sees himself as a hard worker who values effort, is confident in his own abilities and is not concerned about what others think of him.

The attitudes each holds will determine how he behaves. With the first person, winning is an important source of self-esteem. A win will boost his ego, it will reinforce the belief that one can win gambling and increase the likelihood of his boasting to others. A loss will undermine this feeling, resulting in further gambling to recapture the ego boost. For the second, a win or loss will have little impact on his ego, mood or behavior because of his low expectation of winning. He will more readily accept losing without becoming emotionally upset.

In cognitive therapy, the aim is to work out the set of distorted and irrational cognitions – thoughts, attitudes, beliefs – we have, challenge their accuracy, and replace them with more rational and accurate cognitions. Thus the first step we need to take is to identify distorted and mistaken perceptions of gambling. Having done this, we can challenge those perceptions by critically examining what evidence we have to support our views; we are then in a position to replace them with more accurate perceptions. Correcting erroneous and faulty cognitions is another step in the right direction in overcoming problem gambling.

Let us begin by looking at some of the more common irrational cognitions held by people who gamble.

Common Cognitive Distortions and Erroneous Beliefs in Problem Gambling

Gambling: entertainment or a source of income?

A fundamental question to ask yourself is this: 'Does gambling represent a way of earning income or is it a form of entertainment?

162

Gamblers who hold the mistaken belief that gambling is a way of making money will:

- feel bad when they lose;
- chase their losses;
- overestimate their gambling abilities and skills and so take greater risks;
- be prepared to risk more than they can afford on tips or 'certainties';
- become preoccupied with thoughts of gambling;
- gamble rather than work to save money for purchases or payment of bills.

Gamblers who correctly understand that gambling is a costly form of entertainment will:

- be prepared to accept losing in exchange for having a good time;
- not chase losses;
- recognize that gambling involves minimal skill on their part;
- limit the amount of money risked to what they can afford;
- think little of gambling at other times;
- save rather than gamble to obtain needed cash.

Don't be misled by friends who claim that they consistently win. They are still working for a living and are unlikely to boast about their losses. To overcome your gambling, you have to accept the fact that gambling is really entertainment. Essentially, you are paying the gambling industry a fee for the privilege of using some of their facilities to get a sense of excitement and fun. Occasionally they may offer an inducement to continue gambling in the form of a win, simply to encourage you to keep coming back.

'I can win at gambling'

The most prominent erroneous belief among gamblers – and perhaps the hardest to shift – is that you can win at gambling. This fantasy is encouraged by media reports of instant lottery millionaires and big-time casino or race winners, as well as personal experience of winning. True, people can be lucky and have a large win. But examine closely what happens over a period of time. Sadly, most winners return the money through further gambling. Stories abound of lottery winners who, in a very short space of time, either spend or gamble their money away to be left penniless.

I often hear gamblers I have treated say, in referring to a recent large win, 'See, there's the evidence. I won last week, I can do it again.' A nineteen-year-old unemployed adolescent won the equivalent of fifty thousand pounds on a trifecta (picking the first three horses in order) at a trotting meeting in Sydney. Within two weeks, he had lost the lot. He then reported that he 'went out of control' trying to recover his money, and ended up the equivalent of ten thousand pounds in debt, having been convinced, on the basis of one major win, that he could repeat his success.

To examine your own beliefs about gambling and winning, consider the following case.

Trevor has played the slot machines regularly twice a week for the last five years. He invests ten pounds and comes out with, on average, five pounds left in his pocket after each session. At the last session he again started with ten pounds, but halfway through he won a jackpot of a thousand pounds. In his excitement he extended his session, finally stopping when he had only three hundred pounds left in his pocket. Over the next three days he returned and lost the remaining three hundred pounds.

Now, write down your responses to the following questions:

Did Trevor win at gambling?   _____
Did Trevor win overall during the week?   _____
Has Trevor been winning over the long term?   _____

Your answers to these questions will depend on what you mean by winning.

If we limit the time-frame to one session, did Trevor win a

thousand pounds or what he had left at the end of the session, that is, three hundred pounds?

And what happens when we extend the time-frame? If we take into account his performance over three days, can we still say that he won given the fact that he had returned the thousand pounds by that stage?

What about if we extend the time-frame to cover the last twelve months? He has consistently lost 50 per cent of his stake. How much did he lose before winning a thousand pounds briefly – which he then gave back?

Take a few minutes to explore what winning means to you. Focusing on the outcome of a single bet, such as Trevor's thousand-pound jackpot in the above example, will reinforce for you the idea that large wins are possible. This will also foster an impression that such a win places you financially ahead. How many times have you heard someone boast of a large win? What they fail to report is how much they had in their hand at the end of the session. Remember: it doesn't matter how much you win during one session, whether it's a million pounds or more; the crucial questions are, how much did you start with and how much did you finish with? Those are the key facts.

Rather than focusing on individual sessions only, you must monitor your gambling so that you can then calculate your position in regard to wins and losses over a minimum period of twelve months. The longer the time-frame, the more losses you will have. That's the nature of gambling.

Next time someone boasts of winning, ask how much money they lost trying to gain that win. A friend of mine excitedly reported that he had won five hundred pounds on a horse race. His face paled when I asked him how much he had bet and lost in the previous races that day and in the preceding week. His elation turned to dejection when he calculated that he had lost seven hundred and fifty pounds to win five hundred!

The Illusion of Control

Chance plays a central role in gambling. However, many gamblers hold a strong conviction that they can influence the outcome of chance events through their own skilful play. This observation was first reported by E. J. Langer, a researcher who in 1975 carried out experiments which confirmed her hypothesis. She found that people consistently overestimated their ability to influence the outcome of a chance event, even though their skill had absolutely no part to play in determining the final result. We just like to think we have special skills over and above the next gambler.

Take a moment to write down any strategies you follow that you believe give you the winning edge. Review these to see how many are based on real skill and how many are merely superstitious beliefs. To illustrate, gamblers playing craps may throw the dice hard when aiming for high numbers and softly to secure low numbers. In poker, gamblers may arrange the cards in a certain way, slowly revealing the cards one at a time. Lottery players may select favourite numbers. Horse race betters are renowned for having 'systems' which are guaranteed to beat the bookies. In reality, however hard or softly you toss a dice, however you handle the cards, whatever your favourite number or system you employ, none of these so-called skills influences the outcome one little bit.

What are some of the factors that strengthen our sense of illusion of control? Three have been suggested by Robert Ladouceur and Michael Walker, colleagues and international experts in understanding gambling behavior: these are competition, familiarity and choice.

Competition Competition is usually based on the exercise of skill. Therefore, if you challenge an opponent and win, you automatically assume the win to be the result of your personal skill, not of good luck on your part.

Familiarity The more familiar you are with a machine, racetrack or lottery office, the more likely are you to believe that you have control over the outcome. Do you have a favourite slot machine or purchase lottery tickets from a regular agent? Are you drawn to a particular fruit or slot machine because you 'know the spin of the reel'?

166

Active participation and choice   It has been shown that people value lottery tickets that they have chosen themselves over and above those that have been given to them by an agent. So, if you are able to select numbers or tickets, you are more likely to have more confidence in winning.

I have had numerous debates with problem gamblers over the issue of skills and systems. They argue, somewhat illogically, that they have the necessary skills or systems to win, but are prevented from coming out ahead by a run of 'bad luck' or some other reason. They point to a recent succession of wins over a brief period of time, which in their mind confirms their belief.

Take a moment to think about the following points:

- Gambling is not a competition to prove anything to anyone. What does 'beating the system' really mean? Ask yourself, what are you proving to whom if you win at gambling?
- One or two runs of wins does not prove skill or the effectiveness of a system.
- Pure chance with no skill can result in a series of wins.
- If you have the skills to win, can you explain why you are in debt? It is no good explaining that it is due to bad luck.
- If wins are the result of your skill, then losing must also be the result of your skill (or lack of it). Overall, what is your ratio of wins to losses? If you have lost more than you have won, what does this say about your skill?
- Carrying a lucky charm has no impact on chance events, it is only superstitious behavior.

No matter how strongly you hold the cognitive belief that you are a skilful player, the outcome of gambling is determined by chance over which you have no influence whatsoever. The skill of the poker player or horse-race gambler is not in consistently winning but in knowing when to cut their losses.

Biased Evaluation

A phenomenon related to the illusion of control is that of biased evaluations. People do not like to think that they have no skill or ability to pick winners. It makes you feel proud and boosts your ego if others perceive you as a 'skilful' gambler, one who is consistently likely to be ahead, one who knows how to 'read the signs'. So, what do you do when we lose? Easy – you blame someone or something else: the machine is 'fixed', the jockey 'pulled the horse' or the team deliberately 'threw the game'. You take credit for picking winners and dismiss the losses by blaming some outside cause. How many times have you heard fellow gamblers complaining about 'fluke' events that led to losses while boasting of their skills when winning? This biased approach to explaining outcomes means that you tend to remember wins and attribute them to your skills, while losses are quickly and easily put aside and forgotten.

As an exercise, fill in the list here with the last five wins you had. Describe how much, and where, you won. Now make a similar list for your last five losses. Can you remember these as easily?

Wins		Losses	
How much won	Where won	How much lost	Where lost
1			
2			
3			
4			
5			

Try explaining why you lost in each case. Write the reasons down on the list next to the column describing where you lost.

Near-wins

How many times have the symbols on a slot machine lined up for a jackpot except for one crucial reel, your horse lost by a short head, or the lottery result come in just one or two digits different from your ticket? Have you noticed how such 'near-wins' increase your expectation that a win is about due, and how this spurs you on to continue gambling?

Comments often heard from gamblers include:

- 'I'm almost there, one or two more plays and the jackpot must come up.'
- 'The machine is about to start paying, I must keep going.'
- 'Gee, my luck is about to change, I can't stop now.'
- 'Wow, that was close, the next one must win.'

Near-misses, also called 'heart-stoppers', are almost as exciting as actual wins. But don't be deceived. In reality, missing by a whisker is the same as a missing by a mile. It doesn't matter if you needed only the ace on the first reel to win a million or that your horse lost by a nose. The end result is that you lost. More importantly, the results have absolutely no bearing on the next event. Events in gambling are independent. By this I mean that the result of one event has no effect in influencing the next. The roulette spins a number, say 26. The probability of 26 coming up again is exactly the same for the next spin. This occurred to me when I was visiting a casino in Australia with my wife during a conference. I placed a chip on a number which came up. Distracted by a conversation with my wife, I left the chips on the same number which again came up. The same happened again on the next spin. At that stage, we decided that we had won enough to satisfy us, that to continue would inevitably lead to our losing what we had won. So we cashed in our wins and enjoyed a great dinner.

Gambling to Get out of Debt

Look at it logically. Gambling has been the direct cause of the financial problems now facing you. You have gambled for several years and are well behind. What makes you think that gambling is the answer to your problems? What has changed that gives you the idea that you will win now? It is irrational to think that gambling can be a solution to your financial problems when your experience clearly demonstrates that it is the very cause of those problems!

Another, related, erroneous cognition is reflected in the following argument.

'My gambling has caused a major financial problem. I have debts which I cannot pay and I do not have enough money to pay my bills and daily living expenses. I have only a few pounds left which is not going to make any impact on reducing the debt or paying the bills. I owe two hundred pounds but have only twenty; what difference will twenty pounds make in paying off my debt? However, I could win two hundred pounds by gambling that twenty pounds – so why not try? I have nothing to lose. What's the difference between owing two hundred pounds and owing two hundred and twenty? But if I win two hundred pounds, just imagine, my problem would be solved.'

In fact, research has shown that even winning does not solve a gambler's financial problems. Following a major win, gamblers are reluctant to pay off debts. Rather, they reserve the money for future gambling.

'I am on a winning streak. If I continue, I will be able to win enough not only to pay off present debts but also to be able to continue gambling and still have enough to pay bills that are due shortly.'

The inevitable result is that you lose not only your available cash but also your winnings, leaving you in an even worse position.

Even if you pay off the existing debts from a win, within a short time you will repeat the cycle by creating more debts through continued gambling which plunges you back into debt.

Has either of these situations applied to you?

Gambling is an Illness over Which I Have no Control

Many people find it too threatening to admit that they choose to engage in a behavior that causes harm to themselves or others. It is far easier to avoid responsibility by laying blame on some external cause of the behavior, such as an illness or addiction. Frequently heard excuses are:

- I had no control over my behavior.
- The addiction to gambling is too strong to resist.
- I am suffering from a compulsive gambling illness.
- The urge totally overwhelmed me.

Make a list of all the reasons you can think of why you are unable to resist the urge to gamble.

1 _____

2 _____

3 _____

4 _____

5 _____

6 _____

7 _____

8 _____

How many of these reasons are genuine explanations for lack of control over your behavior? I suspect none. It is all too easy to refer to gambling as an addiction or illness under whose spell you are completely powerless: 'Don't blame me, I can't help it, it's not my fault.' This is wrong. Even though your gambling problem may be an addiction or illness (although this is still hotly debated among the experts), this does not diminish the role you play in making your own choices. One cannot argue, as you may with alcohol or drug addiction, that the body has a physiological craving for a substance and it is this need that you are fulfilling. Gambling is not associated with any bodily need, only a sense of excitement. You must admit that you gamble because you enjoy the feeling, because you are stressed or want to escape unpleasant moods.

Think hard: can you identify any virus or bacterium that causes gambling? No; there is no such thing. Gambling is a repetitive behavior that one chooses to engage in despite the unpleasant consequences that result. It takes courage to confront the truth and accept that you are voluntarily giving in to the urge to gamble because you want to gamble even though it may harm you. But once you take this step, you are taking responsibility for your actions and not blaming outside sources. You are now regaining control over your life.

Suggestions on how to Challenge Erroneous and Irrational Beliefs

We have spent some time here describing the types of erroneous and irrational cognitions that some people hold which make them more vulnerable to losing control. Your next step is to learn how to challenge these cognitions and turn them into positive thoughts.

This involves critically examining each thought and considering how accurate it is. To do this, you need to look closely at and challenge the evidence which you think may support your belief. For example, if you believe that you can make money from gambling to pay bills, you should ask yourself the following questions: 'Where is the evidence that I can actually make money? How many times in the past have I actually won and used that money to pay the bill?' or: 'I feel confident that I will win on this occasion, but how many times have I felt this way before and ended up still losing?'

Try challenging some of your thoughts by completing the exercise set out below. Look at the two situations in the example and try to recall the thoughts you had under similar circumstances. Are they rational? If not, why not? What is a more realistic view? Write down a few typical thoughts that occur when you have the urge to gamble in particular situations, and then write down the challenge to them.

Identifying Irrational Ideas; How to Stop Chasing Losses

Situation	Irrational thought	Challenging the evidence in support
1 Finishing a hard day's work and feeling tense and stressed.	I have had a stressful day. To unwind I will drop in and play the slot machines for an hour and no more. I'll gamble five pounds and no more.	How many times in the past have I intended to limit the time and amount gambled but lost control? The end result is that I am more tense and unhappy, not relaxed, after those sessions.
2 Playing the slot machines. Because of a few near-wins, anticipating a win.	There were a number of close calls. Carrying out a ritual such as touching the side of the machine before inserting the coin will improve my chance.	I have carried out my ritual many times before under the same circumstances and it has made no difference.
3 _____	_____	_____
4 _____	_____	_____

The next stage in overcoming irrational thoughts is to replace the erroneous thoughts you have identified with rational, positive thoughts that will improve your sense of self-control and confidence. You should challenge the evidence that leads you to think that you are in the grip of an irresistible urge that you cannot control no matter what. Rather, you should come to realize that you are in fact making a voluntary choice, even though the choice may be a bad one. Let's work through an example. After that, complete the exercise by adding your own examples in the spaces provided.

173

Think back to the last time you were in a gambling situation and the thoughts that were passing through your mind. First, describe the situation.

Situation: Walking past a shop selling lottery tickets and having a strong urge to enter.

Now write down any irrational thoughts that entered your mind, whether they relate to overestimating your level of skill, superstitious behavior or the way you usually talk to yourself in such situations.

Irrational thoughts: The last time I bought a ticket it was only one number off winning a prize. I could win this time. The urge is too strong for me to resist, I must buy a ticket.

What can you say to yourself to challenge these irrational thoughts? Ask yourself, 'Where is the objective evidence to support what I am thinking?'

Challenging irrational thoughts: How many times in the past have I been close and still never won the next time? The result of one draw has no effect on the results of any other draw. Just because I came close to a winning number does not mean that the chance of winning is increased for any future tickets that I purchase. I do have the choice of buying or not buying the ticket; nobody is forcing me to go and buy a ticket.

Now try to substitute thoughts which are rational and reflect reality. What do you consider is the real situation, rather than the situation as you wish it were? What can you say to yourself that will help you realize and accept the truth that you can control your urges and behaviors and make good choices?

Positive thoughts: I can control my urge when I accept that it is my choice to gamble or not. I feel good when I decide to keep the money and not squander it on an unrealistic hope.

Identifying irrational thoughts and seeing them for what they are – false beliefs that lead to bad choices and further suffering from gambling – takes a lot of effort and practice. However, with experience you will be able to challenge erroneous thoughts and substitute positive ones that will improve your self-esteem and ability to overcome your problem gambling. Try the process as described above with some situations of your own in the spaces provided here.

Situation: _____

_____

Irrational thoughts: _____

_____

Challenging thoughts: _____

_____

Positive thoughts: _____

_____

Situation: _____

_____

Irrational thoughts: _____

_____

Challenging thoughts: _____

_____

Positive thoughts: _____

_____

Situation: _____

_____

Irrational thoughts: _____

_____

Challenging thoughts: _____

_____

Positive thoughts: _____

_____

Review of Step 5

This step has addressed some of the different types of thinking errors that gamblers often engage in. By now, you should be aware that the attitudes and beliefs you have held regarding gambling as a source of income, a game at which you can win, a solution to financial problems and a behavior over which you have no control are all erroneous. Remember, the more accurate your perception is of what gambling is really all about, the greater will be your motivation to stop. Do not accept people's boasting at face value; challenge them by seeking more information on their true position in relation to how much they have won or lost overall.

Questioning your own 'positive' views toward gambling will help you eventually overcome your habit. Recognizing that the only real winners in gambling are the gambling industry and the government, who reap the benefits of your losses, will help strengthen your resolve to give up.

Review your progress by answering the following questions:

- Can you identify what erroneous beliefs led you to think you could win in the long term?
- Have you studied the strategies the gambling industry use to entice you to continue gambling?
- Have you started focusing on your losses rather than emphasizing your wins?
- Are you able to challenge your view that gambling is a solution to cash problems?
- Have you accepted responsibility for your own behavior?

If you can answer 'yes' to these questions, you have made further progress toward overcoming your problem gambling.

Preventing Relapses

Once you have learnt the skills described in the earlier steps, you need to maintain the gains you have achieved. This is done simply by regular practice and review, and by anticipating danger signals so that you can act quickly to prevent any recurrence of gambling behavior. The slide back into problem gambling can be an insidious process; outwardly innocent decisions that you make can slowly lead you into high-risk situations. Once exposed to gambling cues, especially if you are under stress and suffering unpleasant emotions, thoughts of having a small fling easily enter your mind. Having one or two small bets can give the false impression that you have full control over the problem and can now safely indulge on occasions without concern. Excuses are made that allow you into more contact with gambling situations, for example by entering gambling establishments with others or by discussing gambling topics in conversations with colleagues. Unfortunately, experience has shown that it is only a matter of time before you find yourself staking more than you intended, or an amount that you can ill afford. This sets off the pressure to have a further bet to catch up. Then comes the chasing as one falls increasingly behind in bills; the downward cycle to relapse has begun.

In this step, you will learn skills in planning ahead and in avoiding risk situations that may precipitate a relapse.

Keeping the Long View

The path to recovery is often bumpy; there are bound to be ups and downs as you struggle to regain control over problem gambling habits. Keep your eye on the overall picture and do not dwell on lapses. Lapses do occur; often they are just individual hiccups, rather than signs of failure and complete relapse. A relapse, on the other hand, is where old habits repeatedly return and take over.

A lapse – that is, a brief return to gambling, be it one bet, a session over several hours or a few episodes of gambling – is a warning sign cautioning you that you need to be more vigilant in practising and applying the skills you have learnt. Re-reading this self-help book and renewing your efforts may be all that is required to get you back into step. At other times, it may be necessary to get straight in touch with your family doctor or counsellor – for example if you are facing additional problems of depression or overwhelming stresses. Do not be despondent in the face of a lapse.

Whether or not you succeed in the long term depends on how you respond to these hiccups. Take the approach that each hiccup is a cautionary warning not to become complacent; when it happens, going through this self-help book again is strongly recommended. I like to use the example of dieting when discussing this point with my clients. Having embarked on a diet, one is invited out to dinner. During the course of the meal, one eats a plate of chocolate dessert. If one feels guilty about this, one may become depressed, seeing it as a complete failure to control the desire to eat sweets, and give up trying any further. The consequence of this is that one will resume overeating and gain weight. A relapse has occurred. Alternatively, one could see the initial event as a lapse and decide that compensatory action needs to be applied; having eaten dessert, plans are made to reduce the intake at the next meal or to exercise more the following day. Planning ahead serves to restore the balance and averts a relapse.

To anticipate and avoid lapses, one needs to:

- be aware of what may cause the return of an urge to gamble,
- understand the series of apparently irrelevant decisions that leads to exposure to gambling opportunities;
- be familiar with the steps needed to be taken to avoid or contain damage.

Guarding against the Urge to Gamble

Generally speaking, urges do not enter our minds suddenly and spontaneously. A number of factors, singly or in combination, may contribute to the appearance of an urge: the most common ones are unpleasant moods and emotions, arguments or conflict with others, and peer pressure.

Unpleasant Moods or Emotions

A gambling lapse can occur in response to the following moods:

- depression, unhappiness or feeling low;
- a sense of frustration in achieving goals;
- resentment at missing out on recognition, praise or promotion for work completed;
- boredom;
- worry and anxiety;
- rejection by others;
- low self-esteem and self-confidence;
- feelings of worthlessness;
- feelings of impatience;
- failure to meet one's unrealistic expectations;
- a sense of failing to achieve one's ambitions.

Which of these apply to you?

For some people, it seems that a swing to elation or euphoria can also be involved, particularly when it is associated with feelings of overconfidence and grandiose ideas that affect judgment.

Interpersonal conflicts

Arguments with one's spouse or partner, family members, friends or employers can create tensions and unpleasant moods, causing one to seek escape through gambling. Gambling is used to discharge tension and as a distraction from pain in much the same way as alcohol or drugs are used to deaden the pain of anxiety. Some common sources of interpersonal conflict include:

- arguments over finances, for example lack of money to buy necessities, go on holidays or buy new items for home or family;
- loss of affection between partners;
- marital sexual dissatisfaction, tension or infidelity;
- criticism of inadequate effort at work or around the home;
- unrealistic expectations;
- being unreliable;
- receiving inadequate attention from a partner – a common feeling following the birth of a baby;
- not getting on with in-laws;
- external conflicts spilling over into one's marital relationship;
- rivalry between peers at work;
- personality clashes with one's boss or colleagues;
- jealousy over the achievements or praise of others.

Again, consider whether any of these applies to you.

Peer and social pressure

Mixing with acquaintances and peers who are active gamblers and who spend a lot of time talking about gambling-related topics is risky. Being constantly reminded of gambling and hearing of large wins by others can gradually undermine your decision not to gamble. Of even more concern is the pressure to agree to invitations to visit gambling establishments.

Ask yourself:

- Do you feel powerless in the face of peer pressure to gamble?
- Do you feel that your acquaintances will laugh or be critical of you if you refuse to participate in the conversation or go with them to gamble?
- Do you fear becoming socially isolated?

It is difficult to control the urge once surrounded by all the glitter and opportunity. It is not in your best interest to protect such social acquaintances at all cost; if all else fails, you may have to face the painful decision whether to continue to mix socially with people who gamble, and so put yourself at risk, or to establish a new circle of friends.

What can you do? The following is recommended:

- Inform your acquaintances of your problem and your decision to stop gambling.
- Ask them not to talk about gambling in your presence.
- Suggest alternative places to go for lunch or a drink. There are eating and drinking places around that do not allow gambling on the premises.
- Ask them to keep an eye on you in regard to gambling. Few things are more effective than knowing others are watching and supervising your behavior.
- Agree to the suggestion that they inform your partner should they spot you gambling.

If your acquaintances ridicule you, or are in any way not supportive of your efforts to overcome your gambling, they are people not worth socializing with. A true friend will endeavour to support you in any way possible, even it means a degree of inconvenience to them. Value these people, because you can turn to them for encouragement at times of need.

Hints on Dealing with Dangerous Situations

Spend a few minutes to consider these mood states, conflict situations and peer pressures and write down a list of possible positive actions you can apply to overcome them. Have a brainstorm session with your partner to see what alternative strategies are available. Think of as many alternatives as possible, no matter how ridiculous or unrealistic they may seem. Write down responses you could make to colleagues who are enticing you to join them gambling. Use your imagination. Once you have exhausted your thoughts, review them and select the ones you believe could be useful. Make a shortlist ranked in order of how important they are to you. Write these down on a small index card that you can keep in your wallet or purse and take out as a reminder whenever you experience one of these moods, conflicts or peer pressures. In this way, you will have the response to the threat immediately to hand.

Avoiding Accidental Exposure to High-risk Situations

It is rare that one will deliberately place oneself in a high-risk situation – that is, one where the possibility of a lapse is greater than normal, for example, visiting a pub where there are electronic gaming devices, or reading a form guide 'just to see who won, out of interest'. Usually, a chain of small and apparently innocent or irrelevant decisions are made that, when put together, result in a lapse. What is happening is that, unconsciously, you are setting yourself up for a lapse. A few typical such decisions are presented below for you to consider. Study these and see which ones are relevant for you.

- I won't gamble, I just want to join my colleagues for a few drinks at the pub.
- I would like to go into the betting shop to test my control. I'm confident I'll succeed.
- I haven't had the urge now for days so there's no problem in my carrying all this cash.
- I've got a few hours to kill, I'll just drop into my favourite club, have a few drinks and watch others play the machines.
- There's no need to rush home after work, I'll drop into the club for a while and unwind instead.
- I want to listen to the race broadcast to see how a horse I know has run its race. I don't care what price it came in at, I'm interested only in its performance.
- My partner and I are arguing. I'll just spend a few pence playing the machines to relax and put myself into a better frame of mind.

It is easy to justify one decision as being totally unrelated to any desire to gamble. There is nothing wrong with carrying around cash in your pocket. There is nothing wrong with visiting friends for lunch. There is basically nothing wrong with watching friends play the slot machines for fun. But put all these together and you have a recipe for disaster. How long do you think you will be able to resist the urge if you are watching others enjoy playing and winning while you stand around with spare cash in your pocket, particularly if you are feeling down in the dumps and under pressure to pay bills?

Review your monitoring sheets to see if there is any consistent pattern in your behavior. Now see if there are any statements that you make to justify your decision to approach a gambling situation, and think of alternative things you could do that would avoid exposure to gambling cues. For example, you could meet friends somewhere else or visit other friends away from a pub or club; you could arrange to meet your partner immediately after work, or resolve your conflict with your partner directly rather than using it as an excuse to start gambling. It is important that you look at each and every decision to pinpoint what the likely outcome might be. In this way, you can recognize the early danger signs signalling the imminence of a lapse.

Hints on Avoiding Unintended Exposure to Risk

On a series of index cards, list alternative actions to follow under all the circumstances you may inadvertently find yourself facing. Describe all these preventive actions in detail, step by step. Learn to be honest with yourself; there is no point in persuading yourself that you can control a situation when in reality you are really setting yourself up for failure. The only person you are letting down is yourself.

Consider whether your motivation is flagging. If you think it is, re-motivate yourself by returning to Step 1 and reviewing the reasons why you should stop gambling. If necessary, resume monitoring gambling behavior more intensely to find out if there are any new stresses you are having difficulty dealing with. A revision of problem-solving and stress management skills (Step 4) can be effective in boosting your ability to cope with anxiety and other negative emotions. Go back to regular practice of the relaxation-based imaginal desensitization procedure (Step 3). Construct a new sequence specific to the new situation and record a new set of instructions. Now go back to

Step 4 and refresh your skills in challenging irrational beliefs and distorted thinking styles.

What Can be Done to Minimize or Contain Damage?

What does one do if faced with an impending lapse? When, say, you have just started playing the slots, begun studying the form guide or purchased a lottery ticket? Stop: don't put in the next coin, place the next bet or buy any more tickets. Take a few minutes' time out to slow yourself down. Take out your index card which has written on it: 'Even though I am happy and confident now, how will I feel WHEN I LOSE?' and give yourself at least three good reasons why you should not continue to gamble. Write these down for future reference if you can.

A note of caution if your goal of treatment is abstinence. Quite often people pursuing abstinence use the proverbial excuse to keep going on, 'I might as well be hung for a sheep as for a lamb', suggesting that the degree to which they gamble is of no relevance. Saying 'I have started gambling, oh well, I might as well carry on now' is absolutely no justification for your behavior. This is the very point at which you must redouble your efforts in applying all the relapse prevention strategies described above.

Once you have got out of the situation, immediately let your partner know of what has just happened. Under no circumstance try to conceal your activity through deceit, covering losses through borrowing or gambling more in the hope of recovering what is lost. Accept responsibility for your error in judgment and the reactions of others toward you. A partner may well be angry at first but he or she will appreciate the fact that you approached him or her for support. In this way, trust will be rebuilt. Most important of all, involving your partner will eliminate any anxiety or pressure on you to gamble as a means of avoiding detection. Invariably, the clients who have responded well to therapy are the ones who have taken the courage to inform their partner, friend or counsellor immediately of any lapse. You will be surprised to see how much worry is lifted off your shoulders once you have disclosed your lapse. But do not abuse this trust and support. A repeated cycle of lapses followed by confessions should raise a question mark over your motivation. If this is happening, be aware that you are manipulating the goodwill of others. A revision of Step 1 is recommended: question your ambivalence or commitment to change.

Review of Step 6

In Step 6 we have considered the importance of anticipating high-risk situations, planning ahead and working out alternative actions to avoid or minimize damage.

- Have you made a list of all the high-risk situations you are most likely to encounter?
- Are you familiar with the chains of individual decisions you make that eventually result in exposing you to such high-risk situations?
- Have you written out a plan of action to follow at any stage when you inadvertently find yourself confronted with an opportunity to gamble?
- Do you know what to say to people who invite or pressure you to join them in a bet?
- Are you in the habit of discussing with your partner or other confidante any urges that may arise, no matter how trivial?
- Are you committed to informing your partner instantly if you have gambled any amount, no matter how small?

If you are confident in answering 'yes' to all of these questions, you are well on the way to maintaining the recovery process in overcoming problem gambling.

STEP 7

How Your Family Can Help

Many gamblers make the mistake of believing they have to struggle to overcome problem gambling on their own. In fact, it is far more effective to work together with partners and other family members in a cooperative manner. Do not underestimate the extent to which you can be helped by the efforts of others in giving you advice, encouragement and recognition and praise for successes achieved. They can provide you with feedback that will reinforce your motivation and maintain your effort in continuing to pursue your goals, particularly when the going gets tough.

If you are single or separated from your partner, you may wish to turn to your immediate family instead. Parents are usually more than willing to help their children overcome problems and are a good source of help. But do not expect to rely on them to solve all your difficulties or to offer you financial assistance to clear your debts. That is an abuse of their position and trust. It is up to you to develop the skills to handle stresses and take responsibility for your financial situation.

Often, gamblers ask parents or partners to cover their debts, that is, to bail them out of a financial crisis in return for promises of repayment. Once the dust settles, the promises are broken and the cycle repeated. Bailing out a gambler is not a solution; it is only a temporary relief at best and at worst an aggravation of the situation. I recall one client who, in debt to the tune of twelve thousand pounds, asked his girlfriend, with whom he lived, to ask her parents for a loan to repay what he owed. This she did, much to his relief. No gambling took place for the next six months; but then, gradually, he succumbed to the temptation and again began gambling small amounts. The inevitable happened. Confident that he was in control, he began to gamble more and more, and his gambling escalated to the extent that twelve months later he had accumulated a new debt of fifteen thousand pounds. The end result of his partner's good intention in bailing him out was that the couple now owed twenty-seven thousand pounds and were forced to sell some assets they had put aside for their future security.

It was clear that my client had limited insight and poor motivation to cease his gambling. Relieved that he was able to eliminate his debt with a further loan from his girlfriend's parents, it became apparent by his attitude that he had not learnt his lesson. I suspect that currently he is on the slippery slope to a third similar crisis. Had his partner remained firm and provided support and encouragement to seek treatment rather than procuring cash, he would have realized the futility of continued gambling and pursued treatment to the benefit of all concerned.

How can your family contribute to helping you overcome your gambling problem? The following suggestions may be useful:

- Communicate openly with your partner about any stress or problems that are facing you. Adopt a policy of trying to solve problems jointly with her/him.
- Do not keep emotions bottled up inside. Obtain feedback and support from your family in learning how to express emotions more appropriately.
- Contact your partner or a family member whenever you experience an urge to gamble.
- Talk about how you feel and allow your partner to refocus your attention on the reasons why you are giving up or cutting back on the gambling.
- Put into place a contingency plan to follow if an urge persists. This may include arranging for a member of your family to pick you up after work to prevent you visiting a pub or club.
- Work out a budget in cooperation with your partner. It may

187

be necessary for you to receive a weekly allowance for a while until you can prove to others that you are trustworthy. Do not feel resentful at this: it is your behavior that has led to this need in the first place.

- Monitor your savings and expenditure and have a regular weekly meeting with your partner to discuss progress. In this way you can receive praise for your achievements.
- Consider ways of limiting your access to cash. Allow your partner to confiscate all your credit cards and cheque books. The idea is not to relinquish all responsibility for finances; rather, you need to convince others that you can control your behavior and can be trusted to meet all your financial commitments. Once this has been accomplished, you can gradually resume responsibility for the family budget.
- If you have gambled, on however small a scale, disclose this to your partner. Again, I repeat that attempting to conceal bets and chase losses to avoid being caught, and the pressure this causes, is the best recipe for failure. Learn to deal directly with failures rather than avoiding them.
- From your monitoring sheets, work out the times of high risk when you are most likely to gamble. Arrange to do alternative activities during those times that will conflict with your ability to gamble. If Saturdays are a bad time, go out to the movies or visit friends. Having something to do will distract you and make it easier to overcome the urge.
- If you have selected controlled gambling as a goal, you will need your partner to act as a supervisor. You must report to her or him each week, showing detailed evidence of the amount you gambled, its source and the outcome in terms of wins and losses. Do not deceive her or him; if you do, eventually you will be discovered and your credibility will be reduced to zero.
- Be prepared, and expect, to have your family scrutinize your every move, to remain suspicious of whether or not you have gambled, and to doubt statements that you are no longer gambling. You cannot blame them for not trusting you; it was your behavior that undermined their trust in you.
- Finally, accept that your family are concerned about you and

that their efforts are all directed toward providing maximum assistance in helping you improve your quality of life by overcoming your problem gambling.

At times, conflict within families over gambling has reached mammoth proportions, resulting in frequent undermining critical comments, arguments and reference to the past: 'It is your fault we have no money, look at how poorly you provide for your family. Even our neighbours on lower salaries do a better job than you. I knew I should have married Joe when I had the chance.' Such comments erode any sense of motivation or self-esteem and make a relapse likely. If there are entrenched difficulties in the relationship, or your partner is showing signs of giving up, it may be necessary for you to consult a marriage or relationship counsellor to address these issues. Threats of separation or divorce should be taken seriously as a sign that your partner has reached the end of her or his tolerance with your behavior. It is up to you to work cooperatively in establishing an atmosphere of reconciliation and, with the joint effort and support of those around you, in overcoming your problem gambling.

A Concluding Remark

Voluntarily to give up an activity that provides so much excitement and dreams of potential wealth is always going to be difficult. But there is no easy road to an easy life. If gambling has created difficulties in your life, you can be sure that continued participation is certainly not the way to overcome these problems. With the assistance of family members and others, you can act to improve the quality of your life immeasurably.

There may well be setbacks along the way, but do not give up hope and motivation. Re-read this self-help book at regular intervals and continually renew the skills you have learnt. Practice is essential if you are to gain mastery over your urges. If you find you need additional guidance, consult your local mental health professional. One or more sessions with a professional can complement the principles outlined in this self-help book and can be an excellent preventive measure to avoid a major relapse.

At no stage should you become complacent and assume you are fully in control and able to resume gambling in the same manner as before. Booster sessions of the imaginal desensitization procedure every six to eight months are recommended as a safety measure.

At all stages be aware that you are overcoming problem gambling for your own sake, but that you are doing so in cooperation with your partner and family members. Seek as much external support as possible. Do not hesitate to call upon your loved ones to provide encouragement and support. Receiving recognition and praise from them will reinforce your resolve to overcome problem gambling.

Finally, use this self-help book as a resource whenever the urge to gamble rears its head, no matter how trivial it appears. Do not dismiss danger signals, for they herald a return to pain.

Useful Reading

Unfortunately, there are few really good books on the treatment of problem gambling outside the field of specialist scientific journals and conference proceedings. Useful material may be obtained from Gamblers Anonymous (see Useful Addresses below) or any of the specialist gambling treatment resource centres that are now emerging in response to the recognition of the widespread welfare and social problems associated with the increased access to gambling in our communities.

For general reading on the subject, the following books are recommended:

D. B. Cornish, *Gambling: A Review of the Literature and its Implications for Policy and Research*, Home Office Research Study No. 42, London, HMSO.

W. R. Eadington and J. A. Cornelius, *Gambling Behaviour and Problem Gambling*, Reno, Nevada, Institute for the Study of Gambling and Commercial Gaming, University of Nevada.

T. Galski, *The Handbook of Pathological Gambling*, Charles C. Thomas Publishers, Springfield, Illinois, 1987.

M Griffiths, *Adolescent Gambling*, London, Routledge, 1997.

E. Hollander, *Obsessive-Compulsive Related Disorders*, Washington DC, American Psychiatric Press, 1993.

H. Kennerley, *Overcoming Anxiety: A Self-help Guide Using Cognitive Behavioral Techniques*, London: Robinson Publishing, 1997. (For a complete list of books in this series, and especially for the titles *Overcoming Panic*, *Overcoming Depression* and *Overcoming Low Self-esteem*, see the series list at the front of this book.)

H. Lesieur, *The Chase*, Cambridge, Mass., Schenkman, 1984.

William Miller and Nick Heather, *Treating Addictive Behaviours: Processes of Change*, New York, Plenum Press, 1986

Jim Orford, *Excessive Appetites: A Psychological View of Addictions*. New York: Wiley, 1985.

M. Walker, *The Psychology of Gambling*. Oxford: Pergamon Press, 1992.

The following more specialist works, are also cited in the text:

John I. Day, 'Horse Racing and the Pari-mutuel', *Annals of the American Academy of Political and Social Science*, 1950, pp. 55–61.

Clemens J. France, 'The Gambling Impulse', *American Journal of Psychology*, 1902, pp. 364–76.

E. J. Langer, 'The Illusion of Control', *Journal of Personality and Social Psychology*, 1975, pp. 311–28.

Virgil W. Peterson, 'Obstacles to Enforcement of Gambling Laws', *Annals of the American Academy of Political and Social Science*, 1950, pp. 9–20.

P. Squires, 'Fyodor Dostoevsky: A Psychopathographical Sketch', *Psychoanalytic Review*, 1937, pp. 365–88.

Useful Addresses

Great Britain

Gamblers Anonymous
Consult your local telephone directory for information on the
nearest meeting.

Canada

The Donwood Problem Gambling Program
124 Merton Street, 5th Floor
Toronto, Ontario M4S 2Z2

United States of America

National Council on Problem Gambling
PO Box 9419
Washington DC 20016

Australia

Gamblers Anonymous
Consult your local telephone directory for information on the
nearest meeting.

Impulse Control Disorders Unit
Psychiatry Research and Teaching Unit
Level 4, Health Services Building
Liverpool Hospital
Liverpool NSW 2170

Lifeline Counselling Services
3/88 Fouveaux Street
Surry Hills
NSW 2010

Wesley Private Hospital Gambling Program
91 Milton Street
Ashfield
NSW 2131

Index

Extra Monitoring Sheets

Daily monitoring sheet

Date: _____ Day: _____

1	2	3	4	5	6	7	8
Time & place	Feelings and thoughts before gambling (rating of tension on ten-point scale – 1= low, 10 = high)	Borrowings	Cash at start of session	Cash at end of session	Win	Loss	Feelings associated with results (rating of tension on ten-point scale – 1 = low, 10 = high)
Total wins/losses & borrowings						Win/Loss: = Borrowing: =	

Daily monitoring sheet

Date: _____ Day: _____

1	2	3	4	5	6	7	8
Time & place	Feelings and thoughts before gambling (rating of tension on ten-point scale – 1= low, 10 = high)	Borrowings	Cash at start of session	Cash at end of session	Win	Loss	Feelings associated with results (rating of tension on ten-point scale – 1 = low, 10 = high)

Total wins/losses & borrowings

Wins/Loss: =

Borrowing: =

Daily monitoring sheet

Date: _____ Day: _____

1	2	3	4	5	6	7	8
Time & place	Feelings and thoughts before gambling (rating of tension on ten-point scale – 1 = low, 10 = high)	Borrowings	Cash at start of session	Cash at end of session	Win	Loss	Feelings associated with results (rating of tension on ten-point scale – 1 = low, 10 = high)
Total wins/losses & borrowings					Wins/Loss: =		
					Borrowing: =		

Daily monitoring sheet

Date: _____   Day: _____

1	2	3	4	5	6	7	8
Time & place	Feelings and thoughts before gambling (rating of tension on ten-point scale – 1= low, 10 = high)	Borrowings	Cash at start of session	Cash at end of session	Win	Loss	Feelings associated with results (rating of tension on ten-point scale – 1 = low, 10 = high)
Total wins/losses & borrowings						**Wins/Loss:** = **Borrowing:** =	

Daily monitoring sheet

Date: _____ Day: _____

1	2	3	4	5	6	7	8
Time & place	Feelings and thoughts before gambling (rating of tension on ten-point scale – 1= low, 10 = high)	Borrowings	Cash at start of session	Cash at end of session	Win	Loss	Feelings associated with results (rating of tension on ten-point scale – 1 = low, 10 = high)
Total wins/losses & borrowings							**Wins/Loss: =** **Borrowing: =**

Daily monitoring sheet

Date: _____ Day: _____

1	2	3	4	5	6	7	8
Time & place	Feelings and thoughts before gambling (rating of tension on ten-point scale – 1 = low, 10 = high)	Borrowings	Cash at start of session	Cash at end of session	Win	Loss	Feelings associated with results (rating of tension on ten-point scale – 1 = low, 10 = high)
Total wins/losses & borrowings						Wins/Loss: =	
						Borrowing: =	

Daily monitoring sheet

Date: _____ Day: _____

1	2	3	4	5	6	7	8
Time & place	Feelings and thoughts before gambling (rating of tension on ten-point scale – 1 = low, 10 = high)	Borrowings	Cash at start of session	Cash at end of session	Win	Loss	Feelings associated with results (rating of tension on ten-point scale – 1 = low, 10 = high)
Total wins/losses & borrowings						Wins/Loss: =	
						Borrowing: =	

Weekly summary

Week: _____

Date: _____

Date	Wins	Losses
Day 1		
Day 2		
Day 3		
Day 4		
Day 5		
Day 6		
Day 7		
Total		